Twayne's Theatrical Arts Series

Warren French
EDITOR

Pier Paolo Pasolini

Pier Paolo Pasolini

Pier Paolo Pasolini

STEPHEN SNYDER

University of Manitoba

BOSTON

Twayne Publishers

1980

PN
1998
A3
P287

Pier Paolo Pasolini

is first published in 1980 by Twayne Publishers,
A Division of G. K. Hall & Co.

Copyright © 1980 by G. K. Hall & Co.

Printed on permanent/durable acid-free paper and bound
in the United States of America

First Printing, October 1980

Frontispiece Photo of Pier Paolo Pasolini courtesy of The
Museum of Modern Art/Film Stills Archive

Library of Congress Cataloging in Publication Data

Snyder, Stephen.
Pier Paolo Pasolini.

(Twayne's theatrical arts series)
Filmography: p. 187–197
Bibliography: p. 182–186
Includes index.
1.   Pasolini, Pier Paolo, 1922-1975.
PN1998.A3P287   791.43′0233′0924   80-14019
ISBN 0-8057-9271-6

Contents

About the Author

STEPHEN SNYDER is a resident of the western portions of the United States and Canada. He first became interested in film study through attending a screening of *The Virgin Spring* for a film club at the University of Idaho. He received a Ph.D. in Renaissance studies from the University of Florida in 1975, where he taught in the film program for three years. He teaches literature and film at the University of Manitoba. He has published essays on writers in American film, the films of Pasolini, and the films of Federico Fellini.

Editor's Foreword

ALTHOUGH Pier Paolo Pasolini's extraordinary career has been mysteriously terminated on a downbeat, his position in film history remains far from clear. Stephen Snyder wisely avoids trying to sum up Pasolini's controversial achievement. It is too early for summary judgments—though some have been forthcoming.

One reason why Snyder is justified in not committing himself to any firm position at this point is that he has enough to do in this study to examine Pasolini's work from one point of view. With whatever distaste or awe film historians and critics may view Pasolini, one must admit that he is one of the most complex and subtle-minded individuals to be attracted from more traditional literary forms to film. No single study can encompass Pasolini any more than it can Henry James, much of whose work remains enigmatic after a century.

Snyder concentrates on what is probably at present the most hotly disputed aspect of Pasolini's art—the relationship between ideology and vision (in both cinematic and metaphysical senses) in his films. Snyder probes particularly the oversimplified portrayal of Pasolini as an allegorist in search of vehicles for projecting an uneasy mixture of Freudianism and Marxism. Snyder's careful analysis of the films' visual qualities refutes this superficial presumption of a mindset that Pasolini himself explained he had abandoned early in his career. What Snyder produces is a guide to *looking* at Pasolini's films; something that we must learn to do carefully before we can hope to do anything else with them.

Beyond this achievement, however, do beckon a variety of approaches that will show us—as such approaches always do—more about the viewpoint of the critics than the subject. Reading this book, I was most struck, for example, by the way in which someone versed in eighteenth-century British literature might perceive similarities between the "excremental vision" in Pasolini's later films and in the work of Jonathan Swift, which might help illuminate Pasolini's intentions, techniques, and achievements. It might not be too fanciful to see Pasolini as a Swift of our century (a speculation that opens up further intriguing questions about what Swift meant to his own times and what it means to be a Swift to ours). Others will find material for comparing Pasolini to other artists of the present and past. Snyder seeks not to place a stone on the premature grave of Pasolini, but to serve, appropriately to the art involved, as a lens through which visions of the man may be brought into focus.

I hope that this book will be able to do its work of inspiring others. The principal danger is that it may have to remain a source of information rather than a stimulant to new perceptions. This undesirable situation is possible, since some of Pasolini's pictures have never been shown in the United States, others are not available for study, and scarcely any has been distributed in a way that might kindle interest in his work. Even inveterate filmgoers may know Pasolini only for *The Gospel According to St. Matthew* and perhaps *Teorema*, as they know Jean-Luc Godard only for *Breathless* and perhaps *Alphaville*.

This comparison of the two directors is more than coincidental. A large part of the problem of the receptions in both Europe and the United States of both Godard and Pasolini is that cultists expected them to go on turning out *Breathless*es and *St. Matthew*s, while the directors refused to repeat themselves, choosing rather to make constantly new and greater demands on the audience. Their artistic and intellectual restlessness has led to disappointment, confusion, and at last resentment. If they are ever to be known, however, as the dynamic artists they have been rather than as creators early in their careers of popular icons, we are going to need to be able to study all their films, not just as autonomous achievements, but also as steps in the development of their careers.

As a necessarily preliminary study of a complex and difficult body of work, this book about Pasolini departs somewhat from the usual plan of the retrospective histories comprising this series. It is basically a series of interrelated essays on Pasolini's major films. It does not deal with Pasolini's formidable accomplishments as a scholar and an artist in media other than film (a forthcoming book in the Twayne World Authors Series will explore these aspects of his career). Also, certain primarily documentary films and brief contributions to compilation films that did not directly contribute to the development of his narrative cinema are not discussed at length in the text, but summarized in the filmography.

W. F.

Preface

I FELT in writing this book that to be of value it ought to supply its readers, many of whom are or will be engaged in teaching film courses, with useful and accessible ideas on the individual films of Pasolini as well as a sense of the organic development of his career. Information dealing with his life, intellectual milieu, and private opinions is readily available in Oswald Stack's book, *Pasolini on Pasolini*. Thus, in the present study I have tried to provide a detailed interpretive analysis of Pasolini's films, but one which is consistent with his recorded views and his life. And while my primary restraints have been those of imaginative interpretation I have kept in mind the complaint that the literary critic Ihab Hassan made some time ago in regard to the overly technical literary criticism of Rene Wellek: "The breed of technicians [Wellek's formulation of criticism] has unwittingly sanctioned may have found a truer consummation of their hopes in the laboratories of Oak Ridge."[1] With the current rage to reduce movie art to a scientific study, requiring the methodology of linguistics and the "certitudes" of psychosociology, one feels, similarly, that the present breed of film critics, fostered on the passion for measurable value in the theories of Lévi-Strauss and Metz, longs for cinematic equivalents to test tubes, Bunsen burners, and laboratory rats. Somewhere it has been forgotten that art is a product of imagination and is appropriated through an act of imagination.

As Pasolini was also a contributor to semiotics at one time (although a prodigal son), one cannot ignore the semiological dimension of his films even though desiring to eschew the bureaucratic jargon that encumbers most semiological criticism. But even Pasolini seems always to have felt that the nature of his creative achievement was largely nebulous, a "measure" of man's visionary capacity to behold beauty rather than his rational urge to measure it.

Another attitude I have tried to avoid is that voiced by one Pasolini critic who said, "Films themselves are no more than textual fragments embedded in a far wider set of discourses."[2] "No more than," a phrase suggesting the individual films have no moral/aesthetic life of their own. This "fragment" view of art strikes me as being a kind of half-truth by which one could easily conclude that, indeed, nothing exists with any integrity outside a wider context. Presumably, the universe is nothing more than a fragment in a wider discourse. Obviously, if we reduce the *Pieta* or the "Emperor Concerto" to measurable centimeters of wider discourse we should be left with a heap of stone and a fragmented pastiche of ideas. But a work of art assumes its unique integrity by the manner in which it "transubstantiates" experience and "discourses" through an irreducibly novel dynamic, thus introducing a degree of novelty into the continuum of human experience. And it is this novel dynamic life force that any critic of Pasolini's work must deal with, being aware that its peculiar tensions are generated from the confrontation of the individual with the demands of wider contexts, larger discourses. I have tried to treat this conflict according to the various guises in which it appears, be it the relationship of art (novelty) and environment (inheritance); religious perception (which sanctions the inviolable integrity of the individual) and Marxism (which asserts his inevitable conditioning by an environment); or simple conformism (total public identity against which Pasolini stormed for much of his life), and individuation, (of which he can also be critical, if it becomes mere egotistical individuality). Probably the most persistent conflict in this series is that between "reason" and "mystery," the latter being associated by Pasolini with an irrational, magical, and wholly experiential wonder of life; the former with mechanical sterility.

The irrational appeal (or nonappeal) of Pasolini's films was no better demonstrated to me than with *The Gospel According to Matthew*. This was the first Pasolini film I had ever seen, attending, in fact, as a way of escaping the heat more than from any desire to see the movie. The audience at this screening seemed composed primarily of fundamentalists, most bearing personal copies of the Bible and arguing with each other over the accuracy of various versions. A tall, bald fellow in front of me kept jumping from his seat, brandishing his Bible like a sword, exhorting all to know that "this is the book, it's all in here." Ironically, within twenty minutes most of these people stormed out, en masse, in sheer disgust, while those of more nebulous religious spirit remained and were quite moved by the film. Clearly, the unsupple preconceptions of the Christians, seeking only a reflection of their personal beliefs in the art work, had so limited their perception as to make them unreceptive to what existed in abundance in the film, a totally nonrational, imaginative moral experience. Many Marxists, seeking a ratification rather than a challenge to their views in Pasolini's art, have suffered disappointments similar to those of the Christians present at the screening of *The Gospel According to Matthew*. Ultimately, then, it is the vitality of his images, common to all of his good films, his commitment to envisionment itself that makes Pasolini's works enduring art, more than their ideology and intellectual organization (which, unfortunately, is the acreage most susceptible to analytic survey in a critical work).

Critics of Pasolini's films have been obsessed with his Marxism or presumed Freudianism, ignoring his criticism of both, and forgetting that his deepest passions were spiritual. These passions amalgamated themselves into a spiritual vision of life which presided over and even shaped his political and psychological opinions. Thus a popular view of Pasolini as an exclusively political filmmaker, defending the ramparts of mystification, has been erroneously fostered. While ideological concerns abide in most of his films, it is, in the long run, the poetic rather than ideological dimensions which make the films interesting. It was essentially the poetic/spiritual side of Pasolini's imagination that I chose to follow, feeling that in the long run this approach would disclose the richest veins in his work.

Pasolini's popularity with audiences has waxed and waned in the extreme. His early films mildly pleased neo-realists and the Marxists while occasionally invoking the wrath of the old establishment (with *La Ricotta* he was convicted of slandering church and state). *The Gospel According to Matthew* restored his favor generally, without alienating too many other supporters. However, with *The Hawks and the Sparrows* and the subsequent works, charges were lodged of betraying "the Cause" (Marxism), promoting immorality, or perpetrating obfuscation. Of his later films, only *Medea* has won much of an audience in North America and only *Salo* is well known, primarily for its shocking subject matter. Ironically, at a time when hard core film pornography can be bought in stalls off the interstate highways, many of Pasolini's finest films (*The Arabian Nights*, for example) have been ignored by distributors because of their scenes of male nudity or some other presumed offense to public taste. Worse, those which are available tend to be ignored because of their assumed obscurity. Pasolini was neither a pornographer nor a cloak-and-dagger obscurantist. The humanistic dimensions of his films are readily available to anyone who will look, and his ideological concerns require little specialized knowledge or political commitment to be appreciated. I suspect, particularly in light of his reputation in Europe, that his noncommercial style has been somewhat ahead of American sensibilities. In this regard, Italian cinema generally has suffered a decline with American audiences in recent years. *Zabriskie Point* was unequivocally disparaged, *Casanova* abhorred, *Roma* unattended, and *1900* lukewarmly received.

Perhaps Pasolini holds no immediate relevance for an American film audience. If so, it is doubly ironic since he envisioned cinema as a universal language free from the mediatory quality of words and free from the chauvinism he associated with literature (i.e., its inevitable classification along nationalist lines because of the language limitation). Film shows only individuals, whose humanity transcends their nationality. One hopes, at least marginally in a work such as this, to illuminate the contours of Pasolini's humanistic vision and thus to increase the general appreciation of an exceptional talent.

Lastly, I would like to deflect the responsibility for inadequacies in the discussion of certain films (*Oedipus Rex, Mamma Roma, Salo,* and *The Canterbury Tales*) which is in part due to absurd distribution problems which restricted me to a single viewing of the works.

S. S.

University of Manitoba

Acknowledgments

I WOULD LIKE to thank Mr. Guido Cincotti of the Centro Sperimentale di Cinematographica in Rome for accommodating my screening needs on short notice; the Canada Council and University of Manitoba for helping me get there; Allison Graham for valuable editorial suggestions; my colleagues, Frank Burke for helpful arguing, George Toles for his mercurial wit, and Gene Walz for his keen eye for Pasoliniana; Professor James Goldsmith for his unearthing of much useful material; Ben Lawton of Purdue University for generating interest and screening films otherwise unavailable to me at the Purdue Conference on Film; Irene Thain and Nancy Lane of the University of Manitoba Media Resources Department for help in locating distributors; Shirley Geller, who, as program director at the University of Manitoba, brought in films and helped translate some Italian; Bill Robinson of the University of Florida for his point of view and vocabulary; Wayne Douglas, whose initial suggestions (go west) contributed providentially to the birth of this project; the library staff of the University of Manitoba for running down several articles for me; Irving Wormser of Peppercorn Wormser for setting up a screening of *Salo;* the various distributors, whose cooperation was vital: Audio Brandon, New Cinema of Canada, Films Inc., and Warner Brothers; and finally, of course, to Warren French for his resuscitating encouragement and promotion of this project.

Chronology

1922   Pier Paolo Pasolini is born March 6, in Bologna, son of a career officer and a mother of peasant origins (Friulan); the family lives in various northern cities as father is restationed.

1937   Begins composing poetry, some of which he will later publish.

1939   Enters University of Bologna, where he meets Giorgio Bassani (the author of *The Garden of the Finzi-Continis*), with whom he will later work, and studies art history under Roberto Longhi. Begins a thesis on Carra, De Pisis, and Morandi but loses his materials during the war.

1942   Evacuated from Bologna to Casarsa, area of mother's origin, where he lives with peasants and publishes first volume of poetry, in Friulan dialect, dedicated later to his father.

1943   Inducted into the army, captured by Germans but escapes. His brother is killed accidentally by Yugoslavian Communists during resistance fighting; his father is made a prisoner of war.

1947   Siding with peasants in their struggle with landowners, Pasolini joins Communist Party for a year, is influenced by writings of Antonio Gramsci, a Marxist, who stresses cultural as well as economic values.

1948   Returns to University of Bologna, eventually completing doctoral thesis on the poetry of Giovanni Pascoli.

1949   Moves to Rome as result of legal problems related to a homosexual incident; poverty forces him to live in the slums.

1950   Secures teaching position in Ciampino area of Rome, but low salary (27,000 lire, or about $50, per month) keeps him in the slums around Ponte Mammolo, which becomes a recurrent locale in his novels.

1951   Finishes first novel, *Ragazzi di Vita*.

1954   With aid of friend Giorgio Bassani, is given work as a screenwriter on Mario Soldati's film, *La Donna del Fiume.*

1955   Publishes *Ragazzi di Vita* ("Children of Life."; in English edition entitled *The Ragazzi*) and is immediately brought to trial for literary obscenity, a situation which works in his favor by bringing him to the attention of filmmakers (Fellini et al.) who admire his ability to capture the jargon of the slum dwellers.

1956   Works as screenwriter on Fellini's *Nights of Cabiria;* although he receives no credit in film titles, the published screenplay honors his collaboration and includes his essay "Notes on *The Nights,*" in which he suggests that *Nights of Cabiria* discloses the direction neo-realism should take, a direction he more or less follows himself in *Accatone* (realism without sentimental patriotism).

1957   *The Ashes of Gramsci* wins Viareggio Prize for poetry.

1959   Father dies. Publishes second novel, *Una Vita Violenta (A Violent Life).*

1960   Acts in Carlo Lizzani's film *Il Gobbo;* Cecilia Mangini directs *La Canta delle Marane*, from a chapter in Pasolini's novel *Ragazzi di vita*, with a commentary added by Pasolini.

1961   *Accatone*, Pasolini's first film, wins praise of critics. Given the Honour Award at Fifth London Film Festival, 1962, First Prize at Karlovy-Vary.

1962   *Mamma Roma*, his second film, is liked less; with *La Ricotta*, an episode in *Rogopag*, Pasolini is convicted of slandering church and state, is reviled at Venice Film Festival. Nevertheless, *La Ricotta* wins Gold Medal by Italian film ciritcs; Paolo Heusch and Brunello Rondi direct *Una Vita Violenta*, from Pasolini's novel of the same title; with Sergio Citti, Pasolini writes the script for Bertolucci's *La Commare Secca.*

1963   *The Gospel According to Matthew* wins five awards at Venice Film Festival plus International Catholic Film Office (ICOC) award for best film.

1964   *Comize d'Amore*

1966   *The Hawks and the Sparrows* praised at New York Film Festival. For his performance in this film, Toto was awarded a special prize at the 1966 Cannes Film Festival. Pasolini acts in Carlo Lizzani's film *Requiescant.*

1967   *Oedipus Rex*, first feature film in color.

1968   *Teorema (Theorem),* awarded ICOC prize, later withdrawn; Laura Betti wins Best Actress award at Venice Film Festival.

1969   *Medea* and *Porcile (Pigsty).*

1971   *The Decameron,* awarded special prize (Silver Bear) at Berlin Film Festival.

1972   *The Canterbury Tales,* wins first prize at Berlin Film Festival.

1974   *The Arabian Nights,* awarded Grand Prize at Cannes Film Festival.

1975   *Salo or the 120 Days of Sodom,* reviled at New York Film Festival. Pasolini is murdered in the early morning of November 2 by Giuseppi Pelusi. Circumstances remain murky.

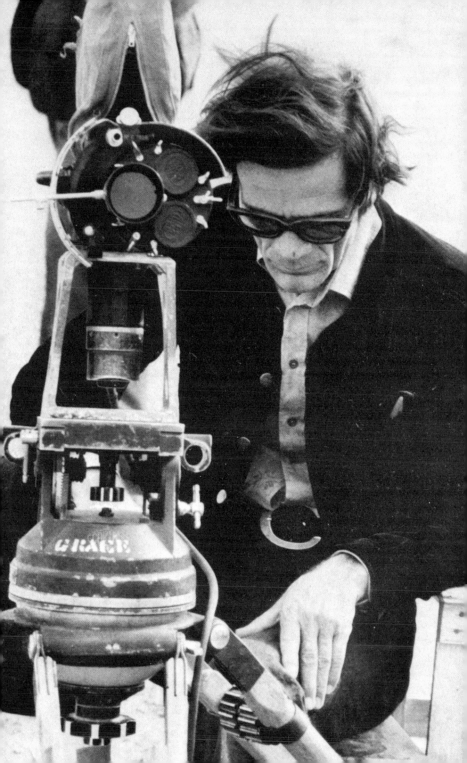

1

Introduction: Drunk on Life

"I SPEND the greater part of my life beyond the edges of the city. . . . I love life with such violence and such intensity that no good can come of it. I am speaking of the physical side of life: the sun, the grass, youth. It is an addiction more terrible than cocaine. It doesn't cost anything and it is available in boundless quantities. I *devour* it ravenously. . . . How it will all end, I don't know . . . ," wrote Pasolini in 1960.[1] The circumstances of his death (a murder) and the scandal of his final film, *Salo* (1975), converged to shape an end as bizarre as it was dark. While, in life, his hunger for the "rough trade" of the Roman slums ended in a violent death, in film, his metaphor of life-as-ingestion ("devour") assumed the monstrous proportions of a last supper of feces. A viewer coming to this last work after having seen previously only *Accatone* (1961), *La Ricotta* (1963), and *Pigsty* (1969), films in which "eating" is a central action, would no doubt marvel at the strange oral obsession of the artist (not to mention the anal fetish, if the viewer had seen *The Canterbury Tales*, 1971) and ruminate upon the unusual path by which the artist's hunger for life had been incarnated in gastronomical visions of gluttony, cannibalism, and coprophagia. The compelling salience of the supper image in its stubborn and variegated reincarnations would suggest it commanded a station of prominence in the imagination of the filmmaker. "I was always a happy gourmand in a fruit garden," he writes elsewhere. "I experienced reality by taking from it."[2] In fact, the dining metaphor does recur in Pasolini's work in a number of contexts, as an expression of spiritual hunger *(The Gospel According to Matthew)*, as an act of assimilation or communion *(The Hawks and the Sparrows*, 1966), as a direct expression of the bodily hunger of poverty *(La Ricotta)*, or as a natural metaphor of the animality of consumerism *(Salo, Pigsty)*.

But what I find interesting about the image is not its tempting promise

19

to unlock the complexity of the films nor the juicy evidence it provides for speculative psychologizing ("oral fixation," etc.) but, rather, its graphic display of the nuclear, organic manner in which Pasolini's imagination operated. The filmic metamorphosis of his gastric metaphor captures the process by which his movies seem to grow out of each other, in the manner of a cocoon opening onto larger, more colorful creatures, each united by a common genetic inheritance, yet infused with novelty and uniqueness. One finds in his films a biological evolution, the later works still enlarging upon the territory opened in the earlier ones.

The sorting out of all the genetic strands involved is hopelessly complicated by Pasolini's insatiable eye and creative energies which sought to ingest all matters of life that came their way. His polymorphic interests provided endless fuel for this.

Pasolini's passion for life seemed destined at times to embrace the entire arena of artistic endeavor. Although known by North Americans primarily as a filmmaker with a flair for the exotic, he is thought of by Italians as an equally significant poet and writer. He was a certified scholar (a doctorate earned by a dissertation on the poet Giovanni Pascoli), a linguist, a nationally honored poet,[3] an author of several novels (two of which hold an international reputation);[4] he was a painter in his youth (originally desiring to write a thesis on art at the University of Bologna); he followed music, wrote both film and literary criticism, produced a weekly barrage of social commentary in a column for the Milan newspaper *Corrier della Sera*, helped to found the review *Officina*, and was an early, though prodigal, promoter of semiological film theory.

Yet in the midst of this prodigious activity, Pasolini seems to have remained, in his phrase, "beyond the edges of the city," outside of the institutions he supported, yet precisely upon the edge of life, unowned by anyone or any system: a man of spiritual perception without a church; an unorthodox Marxist without a party. He surprised many people by criticizing the Marxist student movements of 1968 (the students were the bourgeoisie, the police the real subproletarian victims), rejected their vision of a political cinema, and at various times took pains either to repudiate or to separate himself from an intellectual milieu with which one would normally associate him (the pantheon of Marx, Freud, Levi-Strauss, and Metz).[5] He drew a great deal of fire for his open homosexuality, scandalizing many through his reputed compulsion to seek out the male prostitutes of the Roman subculture; and his own murder, apparently by one such youth (Nino Pelusi), was cast in even greater shadows by the plausibility of Pelusi's story that Pasolini had attacked him—Pier Paolo having been convicted, somewhat earlier, in bizarre circumstances of brandishing a knife at a gas station attendant.[6]

Early Years

While his unique genius must be regarded as native and original, we can see it ignited and shaped by the circumstances of his youth, particularly his evacuation during World War II to Casarsa (in Friuli) on the Yugoslavian border, where he lived among peasants from whose ranks his mother had come. What Pasolini seems to have identified with in these peasants was their very deep and mystical sense of religion which was, in part, pre-Christian and tied to no institution. In speaking of his mother, he described this spirituality as being "purely poetic and natural."[7]

It was through this shared mystical, or holistic, sense of spiritual perception that Pasolini was drawn to fight with the peasants in their struggle against the wealthy landowners and eventually to become a Communist, being at that time unaware of the basic conflict in cosmology between dialectical materialism and his own more spiritual sense of things. To some degree, the inevitable tension between these contradictory perspectives was resolved for Pasolini in the writings of Antonio Gramsci, a Marxist who analyzed cultural as well as economic forces of history. Yet Pasolini's Marxism, while important, remained only one facet of his humanistic gestalt, a function of his artistic and spiritual attitude and not its progenitor. Thus, in response to the question, "Is it necessary to utilize art to build socialism or rather build socialism in order to be free and finally be able to produce art?" Pasolini replied unhesitatingly, "The second alternative is, of course, what I aim for; hence on this point there can be no doubts."[8]

Pasolini's unquenchable love of life allowed his creative nature to flower in depressing conditions which his social conscience condemned. His sojourn in the slums of Rome in the early 1950s, necessitated by his slave wage as a teacher, was converted into two novels and a collection of poems which brought him to the attention of both literary intellectuals and filmmakers. And it was his desire to express as fully as possible this passion for life that drew him to make movies, for they came to embody for him not merely a new technique but a medium in which life expressed itself through itself.[9]

Spiritual Sensibility

Consequently, in trying to understand Pasolini's films, his spiritual sensibility cannot be stressed enough. It precedes and encapsulates his Marxist affinities with the result that his films cannot be approached with the simpleminded assumption that they are, or should be, political statements meant to illustrate Marxist ideology. In most cases, the political dimensions of the films are submerged in the dramatic heart of the narrative. What Pasolini takes from Marx is his criticism of capitalist mentality, specifically its reduction of man to a product, a piece of merchandise. He shares with him, also, the sense that the degree of freedom in a society is largely a measure of the freedom of its women. Thus, there is a strong sense throughout the canon of Pasolini's films that the exploitation of man by man inherent in capitalist economics (at least for Pasolini) begins with the exploitation of women by men. The relationship of prostitute to pimp becomes a defining model of sexual relationships generally. In both *Accatone* and *Mamma Roma* (1962), women are exploited as a means of support for men. It is hard for Pasolini to imagine a story of successful self-liberation which is not also a tale of female emancipation. Thus, his most positive film, *The Arabian Nights* (1974), on the political side, is the story of a female slave who triumphs over a male-dominated world. The exceptions to the rule are *Teorema* (1968) and *The Gospel According to Matthew* (1964). But even Pasolini's Christ is given enough feminine qualities to have promoted one critic to assert that Pasolini drew Jesus to be an obvious homosexual; in addition, Pasolini described the strange protagonist of *Teorema* as being virtually bisexual.[10]

This bisexuality of personality, as manifested by these figures, reveals a significant psychological dimension to Pasolini's work. Although commonly assumed by critics to be a Freudian, primarily because of his film *Oedipus Rex* (1967), Pasolini's concepts of psychology bear equally strong affinities to those of Jung (whose name crops up as often in his conversations positively as Freud's does negatively).[11] That is, throughout his films, Pasolini develops a sense of the human personality as a dynamic interaction of male and female principles, congruent with Jung's ideas, though not necessarily influenced by them. For example, *The Hawks and the Sparrows* contains a latent symbolic tension between male and female in the opposition of the crow (masculinity, sunlight, reason, and consciousness) with the girl Luna (femininity, vitality, moonlight, and mystery). Toto and Nino culminate their education by eating the crow and coupling with Luna in obstinately symbolic acts of assimilating male and female powers. Or consider *Accatone:* the protagonist's development of tenderness, an emotion expressed previously only by his beloved Stella, assumes the proportion of a genesis of feminine powers, an act of growth beyond the meanness of his former male chauvinist mentality. His assumption of femininity is given strong emphasis by Pasolini when he has Accatone unconsciously don a woman's hat prior to his crucial encounter with Stella. The most outstanding example of this sexual congress of personality is the figure of Zumurrud in *The Arabian Nights.* Not only does she dress herself in male "drag" (a metaphor, as one friend suggested, of Pasolini's view of himself), but she employs both "masculine aggression" and "feminine wiles" in her galloping race to kingship and love. She provides, in Pasolini's films, the clearest and most intriguing picture of self-liberation as an integration of sexually opposite personality traits.

Political Ideology

As these examples indicate, Pasolini's artistry is deepened and enriched by tributaries other than political ideology. In fact, one can trace the course of his development through his changing attitudes about the function of ideology in art, beginning with his early "manifesto" of the need for the artist to work from such a basis. In an often quoted polemic, he asserted that "the artist . . . must apply to his work that critical and conscience-minded ideology which will enable him to penetrate the reality of his time, interpreting it through the ideology in which he believes. In Italy, at this moment, I maintain that the only possible ideology is the socialist philosophy, Marxism."[12]

In the years immediately following this statement, Pasolini's Marxism suffered a crisis which left some indelible marks upon it. Probably, as his own statements suggest, he was disillusioned by the unremitting materialism and bourgeois rationalism of many of the Marxists.[13] Hence, by 1964 he notes, "The mystery of life and death and of suffering—and particularly of religion—is something the Marxists do not want to consider."[14] And in an interview with John Bragin he adds, "*Uccelaci Uccellini* [*The Hawks and the Sparrows*] makes explicit the relationship between Christianity and Marxism, practically, the relationship between mystery and reason. Reason answers up to a certain point, but after a certain point it cannot respond, and mystery enters."[15] By 1967 he pro-

claims bluntly, "I want to stress the fact that now, at forty-five years of
age, I have emerged from the wilderness of Freudian and Marxist
dogma."[16]

Pasolini does not cease his attack upon capitalist values, but in his art
political invective (which we can call quasi-Marxist) is submerged
deeper and deeper into the life of the film; ideology "is dissolved in
being. . . ."[17] Despite his injunction on the need to penetrate reality by
ideology, one scours his films in vain for actual delineations of model
Marxist societies. Nor can one find a film in which ideology or a Marxist
community is envisioned, unequivocally, as raising the consciousness of
any individual. The crow in *The Hawks and the Sparrows* makes the
best attempt at this, although even an audience of Marxist sympathizers
breathes with relief when he leaves the film as dinner for Toto. The
obnoxious drudgery of the crow's perfervid chatter is clearly built into
the film by Pasolini's feelings about the limitations of Marxist thought.[18]

The one artistic work in which he unambiguously presents a Communist community in a complimentary light is his novel *A Violent Life*
(1959). Tommaso Puzzilli begins life as a faceless (and, for practical pur-
poses, parentless) child of the Roman slums, where all life seems perpetually saturated with the smell of feces and urine. In fact, one of the
pranks Tommaso and his pals pull for the Fascists is the coating of a
socialist building with excrement. His life is coordinated principally by
the herd mentality of his gang, none of whose members seems to like
each other, yet each of whom depends upon the consensus bravado of
the group for identity. Tommaso, witnessing the slow dissolution of the
group by accident and arrest, begins to develop his own sense of direction (albeit petit bourgeois) through a minor love affair. A stretch in
prison also prods him toward a more complex sense of morality. Eventually, however, he develops tuberculosis and is hospitalized. Motivated
by his growing capacity for compassion and responsibility, he begins to
sympathize with Communist ideals and helps the patients organize a
revolt against their deplorable conditions. His humanitarian instincts,
shaped and fertilized by the Communist Party, draw him into a deeper
involvement with the problems of human exploitation. He dies while
giving aid to slum dwellers victimized by a flood, but his life has carved
a clear picture of regeneration and redemption.

Between the publication of *A Violent Life* (1959) and the release of
Accatone (1961), Pasolini's "ideological world" was "under somewhat
of a crisis."[19] The character Accatone, not radically different from
Tommaso, does not achieve the same salvation Tommaso does, but

finds another sort of personal redemption which is, I believe, more significant. Accatone dies as a thief, but also as a person who has developed the capacity to love. His redemption, while small in terms of socialist yardsticks, is large by virtue of its emergence from within his own soul—opposed, as in Tommaso's case, to its being conditioned by an external system. In this sense, *Accatone* evinces a deeper expression of faith in man than did its literary predecessor. The change in Pasolini's feelings occurring in the time between the two works is not a repudiation of Marxism, but a partial loss of faith in the Communist Party and in the efficacy of regeneration imposed on the individual from an external source. The Marxist community should exist as a symptom rather than a total remedy for health. Without the internal and innate capacity of the individual for spiritual awareness, social change will remain only half effective.

With *The Gospel According to Matthew*, it becomes clear that Pasolini's natural commitment as an artist is less to intellectual abstractions via ideology than to the incarnate spirituality of life itself. "But internally nothing I've ever done has been more fitted to me myself than the *Gospel* . . . my tendency always to see something sacred and mythic and epic in everything. . . . *The Gospel* was just right for me, even though I don't believe in the divinity of Christ, because my vision of the world is religious. . . ."[20] In one sense, Pasolini's achievement in this film is the release of the individual's capacity for a spiritual vision (neither institutionalized nor Platonic) from within himself, by which he keeps faith with the life of this world rather than striving to break from it. Pasolini's Christ is a figure who manifests divinity in his very fleshness: "I followed the Christ of Matthew: . . . a figure who was man and God at the same time."[21] While his Christ has the fire of a revolutionary, he is not redeemed by a system (as Tommaso is) nor does his spirituality operate as a reaction to the squalor of the world as an urge to escape from it (as is Accatone's). He is holistically integrated, a measure of the capacity and urgency of Pasolini's imagination to apprehend precisely such a vision.

A Holistic Sensibility

As a corollary to the transition from environmental to self-generated salvation in these works, there is an important shift in style, a trend by which the protagonist is "sanctified" less by imposed techniques than by his very presence. Pasolini notes that "In *Gospel* I completely liberated that religious element of *Accatone* which was implicit, which was in the style."[22] And he proclaims in another interview that he let the story tell itself, so to speak: "I could not tell the story of Christ—making him the son of God—with myself as the author of the story, because I am not a believer. So I didn't work as an author."[23]

The spiritual element liberated in *The Gospel According to Matthew* is not necessarily that of fundamentalist Christianity which perceives man only as a fallen creature in an arena of toil, whose salvation lies in detaching himself from earth to fly to an abode in the sky. Because he is both God and man, Pasolini's Christ is an affirmation of the director's own commitment to life and, hence, to the concrete world: "The passion that had taken the form of a great love of literature and for life gradually stripped itself of the love for literature and turned to what it really was— a passion for life, for reality, for physical, sexual, objectual, existential reality around me. This is my first and only great love and the cinema in a way forced me to turn to it and express only it."[24]

What Pasolini proclaims is that the world itself, despite its surplus of misery and toil, is a spiritual event, and the capacity to perceive this transposes that world in a new light: "But is 'being' natural? No, not for me; on the contrary to me it seems wonderful, mysterious, and, if anything, absolutely unnatural."[25] "My view of the world is always at bottom of an epical nature."[26] As a consequence, the recurring motivation behind his films "is to give back to reality its *original* sacred significance."[27]

As the quotation suggests, reality in Pasolini's vision is a holistic event—a unified process in which the distinctions between spirit and flesh, or the denial of either, emerge as symptoms of a withered imagination, a contraction of psychic life, a fragmentation in the soul which manifests itself as a desire to retreat from a confrontation with the total mystery of existence. Dualisms become symptomatic of a disease which wishes to control reality by narrowing its dimensions to manageable units. This disease constitutes the actual "fall of man" in Pasolini's works, the progenitor of the conditions of human misery.

Holistic consciousness is thus probably the most inclusive concept one may apply to Pasolini's work as a means of appreciating its opulence. In some manner the events and images which preside over his work—eating, sexual integration, seeing—receive special ordination from his sense of the crucial nature of holism in human development.

Of special significance in his holistic sensibility is the role of the eye, for through it man "devours" his world, as it were, not only apprehending but participating in the plenitude of his universe. (One thinks of the

Bunuelesque cutting of the eyes in *Salo* or the prominence of visions in *The Decameron*.) Significantly, when Pasolini speaks of his religious frame of mind, it is always in terms of "seeing:" "My way of *seeing* the world, which is perhaps . . . too reverential"; "My tendency always to *see* something sacred. . . ."[28] And he makes the unitive power of images themselves explicit at various times: "The cinema . . . is more than anything visible, it's images. The connection with the world in cinema is closer, more personal, more emotional than in any other art."[29] Ultimately, seeing assumes the value of a creative act in the films, an aspect of man's ability to envision the possibilities of love and freedom, as well as an expression of his immediate existential connection to the world.

Although poetic in expression, Pasolini's celebrations of life have caused problems for some critics. If there is no difference between art and experience, there arises the obvious question as to why bother with art. Pasolini's answer to this seems simply that our art forms often provide us with more intense penetrations of reality than our standard waking consciousness admits, but for someone of his sensibility there must inevitably come states when the distinctions between life and art dissolve in a current of heightened consciousness. On the one hand, he can assert that "the main characteristic of the films I make is to put something 'real' on the screen, but something the spectator has become unused to seeing";[30] and on the other, he can condemn naturalism as an artistic form.[31] But what Pasolini means by naturalism in these references is the specific literary movement fostered by Zola which reduces life to a purely materialistic machine. Outside of this context, naturalism assumes a slightly different significance as an aspect of reality from which the bourgeois mind shrinks through the pursuit of refinement: "But where does all this fear of naturalism come from? What does this fear hide, if not reality itself? And isn't it bourgeois intellectuals who are afraid of reality?"[32]

Partly as a means of distinguishing aesthetic from normal experience, Pasolini launched himself into the study of film semiology, the results of which it is not my intent to treat at length in this book. Suffice it to say that his conclusions stress the oneiric and irrational contribution of the artist to his material and, literally, his power to let the mystery of life reveal itself. The sense by which cinema is a "language" becomes matter for speculation in all of this: "What is the difference between the cinema and reality? Practically none. I realized that the cinema is a system of signs whose semiology corresponds to a possible semiology of the system of signs of reality itself."[33]

We seem to be turning in a slow ellipse here, for when the world itself is conceived of as a language the utility of the semiological concept can be somewhat erased. Pasolini tends to use the words "sign" and "language" almost metaphorically, as convenient analogies rather than literal descriptions of the texture of consciousness. Consider this mystical assertion: "Things in themselves are profoundly poetic: a tree photographed is poetic, a human face photographed is poetic because physicity is poetic in itself, because it is an apparition, because it is full of mystery, because it is full of ambiguity, because it is full of polyvalent meaning, because even a tree is a sign of a linguistic system. But who talks through a tree? God, or reality itself."[34] It seems clear to me that Pasolini is using the idea of language as a figure of speech, for the sense in which God speaks through a tree is not as a linguistic code to convey a practical definition—the recognition of the tree as an object in space *rationally* apprehended as distinct from a rock is of lesser significance than the spiritual beauty it manifests. God manifests himself as an aesthetic experience which is meant to transcend the limits of the rational mentality (which possesses the tree by naming it) for a more immediate and profound participation in "pure being."[35] These "messages" can have no dictionary, for in order to be authentic they must be new, and it is in the experience of renewal that Pasolini finds the "meaning" of his creative endeavors: "I do this, as do all writers and authors, out of the need for authenticity. And it is clear that authenticity is always new. It is born of previous examples, but if it is authentic, it supercedes these and destroys them."[36] Consequently, the elements which transmit the authentic experience can never be found in a "dictionary"—all of which is a roundabout way of saying what is common knowledge, that art is not accessible by methodology because it is not a discourse of truth but an imaginative experience which requires an act of imagination like that of the artist to be fully appropriated: "My vocation is literary and artistic, and thus beyond being simply ideological."[37]

In the end, the distinction between art and life is probably unimportant since the motivation for creative action is to a degree beyond the conscious control of the artist. He either "has it" or he doesn't: "What is it that urges me to create. . . . There is this same feeling I have never gone into deeply. I began to write poetry when I was seven years old, and what it was that made me write poetry at the age of seven I have never understood. Perhaps it was the urge to express oneself and the urge to bear witness of the world and to partake in or to create an action in which we are involved, to engage oneself in that act."[38] What distinguishes the aesthetic experience from "normal" consciousness is the degree of intensity in the act of the imagination involved on the part of both artist and viewer, the particularly subjective expression of a concrete imagination which distills life from one process to another. And what moral benefit is involved? Again, it is not measurable; but using Nur Ed Din from Pasolini's *The Arabian Nights* as a model, it is the education of the soul to a greater awareness of the possibilities for love. So ultimately, for Pasolini, the cinema is an act of love which confirms man's creative spirit to be not only a part of life, but the power within life, a measure of his capacity to love. Filmmaking becomes an erotic act of love: "Shooting films is a little bit like a drug for me. It's like being drunk on reality. I like it so much in an erotic, panicked, or . . . religious way. When I make a film I am in reality and I make reality."[39]

Drunk with life and infused with Marxist philosophy as well, Pasolini was naturally inclined to view reality as a process of inevitable change rather than as a static structure. The confluence of his spiritual conscience with his Marxist education, however, resulted in a vision of process and historical change which is not defined exclusively by the idealistic logic of dialectical materialism. Change is more irrational and violent in Pasolini's vision than in Marx's, capable of erupting mysteriously without precedent. In three films from the middle of his career (*Oedipus Rex*, 1967; *Medea*, 1970; *Teorema*, 1969) he composed a history of human consciousness, revealed as a process of radical transformations. These leaps are "quantum," lacking the strict continuity enshrined by classical physics. Their source—that of art itself—presides existentially over all attempts to know it, ordaining life with a destiny beyond the desire of reason to grasp the absolute: "Reason answers up to a certain point, but after a certain point it cannot respond and mystery enters."[40]

If reality is indeed a process rather than an absolute form lurking as a Platonic structure behind the surface of our experience, then all the securities of our "self-evident" certitudes—control, honor, and possession—are indeed illusory. Those who resist this truth, as Medea does, must destroy themselves.

Pasolini's emphasis on radical change as the heart of life poses problems for his critics, for it means the critic's task is not one of illuminating "static" symbolic structure, but, rather, of disclosing "process." "I disagree with the French structuralists however much I admire someone like Levi-Strauss. And in fact the conclusion of my article was to abandon the word 'structure' completely and use the word 'process' instead, which implies the word 'value.'"[41] And in another place he asserts: "By studying the cinema as a system of signs, I came to the conclusion that it is a non-conventional and non-symbolic language, and expresses reality not through symbols but via reality itself. . . ."[42]

Ultimately there can be no holistic apprehension of life that is not the apprehension of process, for the structuralist sensibility implies the reality of hidden, permanent form which must be perceived cognitively and thus abstractly. Reality then splits into the dualistic opposites of mind and body, the latter being merely a temporal illusion covering the permanent truth. The total materialist view of change, on the other hand, ends by reducing life to a mechanical passage.

In his cosmology of the soul, Pasolini's process-consciousness engenders a vision of the "self" as pure potential which, in fact, exists only as action; in terms of the artist's medium, self, like art, is a narrative act, and it is for this reason that narration flourishes in the "Trilogy of Life" (*The Decameron*, 1970; *The Canterbury Tales*, 1971; *The Arabian Nights*, 1974) as both the subject and the substance of the creative act: "The protagonist of the stories is in fact destiny itself, understood, however, as normality, as the essence of every occurrence . . .";[43] "To me it represents an entry into the most mysterious inner workings of the artistic process, an experiment with the ontology of narration, an attempt to engage with the process of rendering a film filmic. . . . I wanted to approach the irrational as the revelation of life which becomes significant only if examined as 'dream' or 'vision.'"[44]

2

Accatone: Love, Merchandise, and Conformism

ALTHOUGH *ACCATONE* is Pasolini's first film, it furnishes a viewer with a virtual anthology of the artistic vision expressed in these lines. Most issues germane to his later films—holistic consciousness, self-indenture, the inability to love—find expression here. Moreover, Pasolini's stylistic proclivities (the preference for wide-angle lenses and distaste for process shots) and his intuitive capacity for wedding theme and style are well realized.

The film is a story of growth in a man who awakens from his slumber as a flesh merchant to the awareness of, and need for, a kind of love which can redeem his arid life—a life blighted through his scorn for spiritual value in human contact. In "L'appennine" Pasolini wrote "—in the eyes—the hardened laugh/of the tenements starved of love."[1] As a pimp, Accatone plies a trade which, by nature, reduces love from an animate power to a marketable product. This condition, of course, defines for Pasolini the basic fault of capitalism, and he tends to see the marketing impulse fueling human relationships generally. They become forms of prostitution, fostering and fostered by the structure of society, in which the individual sells himself or seeks fulfillment in servitude to others rather than through his own power to love. Of particular importance is the ubiquitous indenture of women to men; this relationship becomes both the cornerstone of capitalist society and the symptom of the male's repression of the female side of his own personality (a repression of affection, intuition, and receptiveness).

Still, *Accatone* is not, strictly speaking, a political film. While it connects economic conditions with suffering, it suggests that the origins of human desolation lie within the consciousness of each person and that its cure only begins with the awakening of the individual to the presence of spiritual energy in the physical world. The incapacity to love embod-

33

Franco Citti in Accatone: *the struggle for individuation.*
The Museum of Modern Art/Film Stills Archive

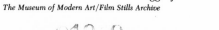

ies a failure in perception, an inability, or refusal, to see the holistic nature of life, the convergence of spirit in flesh, of becoming in being. Ultimately, the issue of holistic consciousness, as an index of Accatone's capacity for love and growth, underlies and sustains the entire narrative. By way of this concept, one may better understand the inevitability of his tragic end; for while he strives, in his love for Stella, to grow beyond a brute materialism, his nascent spirituality lapses gradually into the service of his fear of life, becoming a desire to escape from the physical world entirely, with its daily round of sorrows and demands. A denial of material reality replaces his previous disdain for spiritual value, and results in an equally unsatisfactory state of unfulfillment.

Individuation/Conformism

But Accatone does find in himself some capacity to love and as he does so he becomes more individualized. Because it expresses the pressure of an inner life, love becomes a catalyst of personal growth. Thus, the process of individuation, the story of growth, is the dramatic center of the film and genetic dynamo in which the issues of love, prostitution, and holistic consciousness coalesce. Generally, in the world depicted in the film, the annihilation of love through prostitution engenders a predatory struggle for material supremacy that further undermines human relationships. Predation ultimately makes membership in a group necessary for survival, yet vitiates the possibility of trust between individuals: on two occasions Accatone tries to con his own pals out of a meal at the risk of expulsion from their ranks. As most of his fellow predators are forced back upon the resources of their own consciousness, they are drawn by fear into the orbit of a group identity in whose illusions they find a refuge and release from any discomforting sense of responsibility to others and themselves. Unlike his friends, however, Accatone struggles to grow as an individual through assuming responsibility and opening himself to the promise of a love not reduced to the status of a consumer product.

The process of Accatone's individuation is prefigured in the film's opening episode; in fact, this process informs the structure of most of the episodes of the movie as well as that of the entire plot. Beginning as an anonymous face in a group of lounging men, he quickly singles himself out by starting an argument. This quarrel develops into a wager between Accatone and the group over his ability to swim the Tiber on a full stomach. In fact, the altercation is a ruse on his part to get a free meal. By translating his words into actions, and, in a sense, assuming the responsibility of his calculated brashness, he progressively separates himself from his flock of friends until he stands alone atop a bridge from which he will jump. The low-angle shot employed here even diminishes the sense of background, which might detract from his visual individuation.

The thrust of the scene toward the individuation of Accatone is also captured in the rhythm of the editing. While he is totally submerged in his pack of associates in the opening shots, he emerges from being a face in the crowd to solitary prominence gradually in a series of shots alternating between the character Fulvio and the group. He moves from an anonymous figure in the corner of the screen to sole occupant of the frame.

While the structures of this opening episode conspire to impress upon us the prominence of the individuation impulse in the personality of Accatone, they also intimate a crucial problem in that development. Specifically, in this scene his differentiation leads him relentlessly out of the world rather than into it; visually, he spirals upward and hence outward, causing his ultimate return (literally, the jump) to be fraught with danger. Motivated by the simple desire to escape life, Accatone's extrication of himself from his herd leads him to a dead end of self-conscious isolation (or at least, taken as a model of his experience in the whole of the film, the scene strongly promotes this idea). In fact, it becomes progressively evident in the course of the film that Accatone's struggle to attain freedom in love will be hampered by an ineluctable urge to split himself off from the world while severing ties with his loveless, reptilian acquaintances. Appropriately, at the apex of his self-definition atop the bridge, Accatone is flanked by statues of angels with heads turned to the sky, poised as though ready to vault into the ethereal void.

If the opening episode colors Accatone's individuation with shades of dolor, the second major episode (despite revealing more of Accatone's ugliness) brings into sharper focus its essential moral superiority to the conformist group mentality of his peers. Accatone returns from his successful plunge to learn that his whore, Maddelena, has been incapacitated by a motorcycle accident. With the temper of a sadistic tyrant, he berates her until interrupted by the arrival of Don Salvatore, a friend of Maddelena's former whoremaster, Ciccio, recently imprisoned. We learn in an aside that goes undeveloped that in Ciccio's absence, Accatone, with something approaching charity, is helping to feed Ciccio's wife and children. Our disgust with him is somewhat mitigated, but more important, a clear difference emerges between Accatone and Don

Salvatore. As they drink wine, Accatone becomes a maudlin, blubbering wretch, while Don Salvatore, "the biggest pimp in Naples" (Maddelena's phrase), remains cool and in control. Yet it is precisely his passion for control, which he wields over others, that makes him a sinister and unregenerate model of all that is wrong in his society. With a heaviness akin to his ponderous frame, he seeks to solidify his sense of security through reducing others to extensions of his own will, his own ego. He even finds religion useful, for while Accatone bemoans the profession of pimphood, Don Salvatore justifies it with references to the Virgin Mary, managing in peculiar fashion to disown any responsibility for his exploitative nature. In fact, backed by the assurance of his group of friends, he disowns responsibility for anything, blandly placating himself with the words, "We're all in God's hands together." Obviously, the Don's life is founded on an incredible moral contradiction by which God sanctions slavery, but what is also essential to it is its total group orientation. Apparently, the Don cannot function alone; he must be engulfed in his gang not only to feel out Accatone, but to thrash Maddelena as well.

This suggestion, that these people have no ability to live by themselves, is reinforced by the presence of another group of younger men in the winehouse who openly brag of their recent beating of a whore. If individuality has its pitfalls, the herd mentality is shown to be intimately bound up with cowardice and the misuse of people; having little sense of their own interior reality—of their personal responsibility—the gang members have no respect for it or recognition of it in others. Hence, women are reduced to an alternative of stereotypes: the whore or the saintly mother (Maddelena and Ciccio's wife, respectively), one of the several dualistic fractures latent in human perception in this film.

The degree of Accatone's evolution beyond the social norm comes to light in his capacity to relate to a member of the opposite sex in a manner not based on the master/slave model so distinctly drawn for us by Don Salvatore. Accatone meets Stella almost by accident; she is cleaning old bottles in a junkyard area where Accatone has come in search of his estranged wife, Ascenza. Stella has a lightness and innocence about her, and perhaps it is this which attracts Accatone; very likely it is her innocence with which he falls in love. But Stella, with the purifying touch of her occupation, has a cleansing, even transforming, effect on Accatone. Through his love for her, he develops virtually a new identity, even assuming in her presence a different name, Vittorio. He ultimately frees himself completely from pimping and tries briefly to "plunge into" the currents of necessity by taking a "real" job.

His pilgrim's progress is somewhat halting, however; despite his love for Stella, he responds to her affection by trying to turn her into a whore. He places her on the streets to solicit trade, but repents, retrieves her, and seems truly on the verge of a breakthrough in consciousness.

Accatone's growing individuation is displayed in both his public and private lives. With his brother's aid, he takes a job of hard labor (loading iron rings). As with his dive earlier in the film, he attempts to confront the brute physicality of existence, and this assumption of responsibility alienates him, once again, from his former friends; passing them when returning from work, he bursts into open conflict with them, heaving a shoe at his old cohorts. While his severance is surely a step forward, his show of violence is just as surely a mark of his continued unwillingness to accept wholly the realities of life which impinge upon him. He remains to some degree a child, a fact Pasolini underscores by having a child clasp Accatone after his brawl.

Although outwardly in conflict with the world, inwardly Accatone experiences a fuller awakening of his soul. This activity of his inner life is revealed to us as a burgeoning of his capacity to dream. Returning from work in a state of exhaustion induced by labor and combat, he collapses in a stupor and dreams prophetically of his own destiny. In a significant sense, he is imagining (literally imaging) his own identity from the creative centers of his psyche.

In the dream, he finds himself crossing a bridge, in transition between stages of spiritual growth. He hears himself called to by Don Salvatore, a petition from the vestige of his former identity. But when he approaches the Don, a wall collapses, killing the Pimp of Naples along with his cohorts. The funeral which follows, consistent with the identity link between Accatone and Don Salvatore, is Accatone's, not the Don's. Accatone attends this funeral, passing unrecognized by his friends, for he attends as "Vittorio," the new man. However, this Vittorio is never completely born, in either the dream or the world of daytime consciousness. The new man is unable to break cleanly from the cocoon of the old. Thus, in the dream, Vittorio merely climbs the cemetery wall to stand by Accatone's grave. The dream ends as he looks heavenward; the camera looks with him into a broad, spacious vista. In this expansiveness, one cannot help but feel a sense of freedom, yet within the context, it is a freedom found in release *from* the world rather than *within* it—the freedom, in other words, of death.

Accatone/Vittorio awakens from his dream and reenters the world, but he comes neither as the new man nor entirely as the old. He returns neither to his own slave labor job nor to the enslaving others, but to thievery. He relies on two old acquaintances here, Balilla and Cartegene, figures earlier seen in the winehouse but not closely associated with Accatone. While thievery may not seem much of an advance beyond whoremongering, there is a crucial difference: specifically, larceny may hurt others but it is not based upon the systematic reduction of humans to consumer products. Although in a somewhat perverted sense, the thief, unlike the pimp, must realize in actions the deeds the latter need only imagine abstractly.

When the group is caught by the police, Accatone, consistent with his will toward individuation, leaps onto a convenient motorcycle and flees. And, of course, consistent with the desire to escape always lurking in his individualizing struggle, he is indeed trying to escape something even as he asserts himself. His powers to move have been radically enhanced but are still thwarted by an appetite for evasion. It is tragically appropriate that his final adventure ends with his collision with a truck, an extension of the hard, material core of the work-a-day world. It is the rock against which his powers of growth flounder and end in frustration.

Dualism

When accosted by the police, Accatone and his friends are pulling a cart in which they have concealed a large haunch of ham under a bouquet of flowers. The radical polarity of these objects, lightness versus mass, aesthetic inutility versus utilitarian necessity, typifies the kind of dualistic divisions which proliferate in the film and may well serve as the underpinning of Accatone's unfulfilled life. In their most relevant symbolic posture, the objects present us with an image of disunified spirit and flesh: the meat being literally flesh, the flowers the embodiment of aesthetic, spiritual form whose blossoms serve no physical function, but provide, rather, food for the imagination (they are, in fact, from a bunch which would be sold to the church). This separation of spirit and flesh, the nonholistic perception of the world, defines the fault not only in Accatone's growth process but in his society's structure as well. This fragmentation of vision is a negative matrix which engenders most of the evils in the film in one way or another. Its presence inhabits the world of the film like endless permutations of an equation. For example, the aforementioned stereotyping of women as practiced by Don Salvatore is essentially a distinction between women of spirit, mothers for whom Mary is the archetype, and women of flesh, whores on whose backs the men make a living. The polarity between the two is almost iconically figured for us when Accatone, at Ciccio's house, stands between the prostitute Maddelena and the mother/saint (Ciccio's wife), with her pellucid purity and a child bundled (one is tempted to say "swaddled") in her arms. That women become restricted to these rigid paragons is in part a result of the fact that men choose to see them this way, and the men do this because it is the way in which they have chosen to see their world—a vision in which spirit and substance may be permanently consigned to nonoverlapping realms. The advantage in so perceiving things is that it provides one with a ready excuse for not acknowledging the reality of either, thereby excising one's responsibility to deal with it.

As suggested earlier, there is surely a certain escapism in Accatone's love for Stella. She seems, indeed, to be the soul of innocence. When Accatone first meets her, she is cleaning bottles, removing earth from them. When taken for an automobile ride, she founders in total surprise (although contrived) upon learning that the women who line the road are soliciting sexual customers. Her very name, Stella, associates her with a heavenly otherworld, and although well-rounded like a figure from a Rubens' painting, there is a definite lightness about her. As well as being blond, she is positioned, usually, in a way that allows the light to gather about her hair. Even among the field of debris in which she works, her form is flanked by rows and stacks of translucent bottles whose glistening cleanness conveys the sense of heavenly dissociation from the material world.

Accatone's own desire to extricate himself from the hard mass of reality—which leads him to worship in Stella his own desire for heaven—is implicit in his occupation of pimp, for clearly such a job allows one to deal with necessity through a mediator, rather than confront it directly. Accatone is afraid of life, afraid of the physical struggle, afraid of the humiliation he associates with lowly, but honest, labor. Like that of Mamma Roma, the heroine of Pasolini's next film, Accatone's comportment discloses a disdain for the commonality of life, for physicality itself; through fear of losing himself in life, he shrinks from it toward a nebulous limbo uncorroded by the weight of physicality. On the simplest level, he avoids work, preferring to swindle his friends. He contrives a confidence scheme with Fulvio to secure for themselves a pot of spaghetti which the church has supplied for his cronies. Fulvio starts a fight ("I work and you don't") with the group which forces them to forsake the spaghetti to preserve their sense of honor. Their behavior is a perfect example of the "Platonic problem" they all suffer from, intangible

A predator (Franco Citti) captured by the church [from *Porcile*]
The Museum of Modern Art/Film Stills Archive

abstractions (honor) being accorded a higher value on their "reality scale" than the physical necessities of life. Interestingly enough, Accatone never consumes this food he has so cunningly secured because on his way back to it he encounters Stella and discovers that it is more important to accompany her to a pawn shop, where she will retrieve, appropriately, her father's holy medal. In fact, after the first scene, as he waxes ever more spiritual, Accatone partakes of no solid food. Even when drinking wine with Don Salvatore, the effect of so much indulgence is a drunken stupor. One may say with accuracy that Accatone has a problem assimilating the physical side of life, a problem which limits his growth, undermines his capacity to love, and colors his waking consciousness with somber tones.

Probably the most clear-cut evidence of Accatone's developing servitude to Platonic, nonmaterial aspirations is provided on a purely visual level in a scene with Stella. As the two stroll through an open square, Accatone stops to profess his love for her. He stands directly in front of a church on whose wall stands the portrait of a saint ascending heavenward; it seems to emerge from Accatone himself.

Accatone (Franco Citti) with Stella (Franca Pasut)
The Museum of Modern Art/Film Stills Archive

Insofar as his infatuation with Stella is colored by his aspiration to deliver himself from materiality (which by no means completely tarnishes his affection), Accatone prostitutes both Stella and his love. He

Left: Accatone (Franco Citti) with the little "Madonna" (Adele Cambria)
The Museum of Modern Art/Film Stills Archive

makes of her a symbol of his desire for a haven of tranquillity. One might say, although with some trepidation, that in moving from Maddelena to Stella, Accatone has supplanted one form of prostitution with another, each united by his passion to flee life or, at least, any responsibility for living.

There is one figure in particular we might mention here who quite literally incarnates the loss of love through its profanation. That character is Amore, whose name, by its direct reference to love, endows her with an almost symbolic status. She first appears in the scene dominated by Don Salvatore's revenge on Maddelena. While she postures as a cynical, disillusioned woman of the world, Amore literally breaks down when ditched by a customer whose regularity she has mistaken for real affection (when, in fact, it is affection for a consumer product). She clearly does not understand the logic of merchandised love any more than Accatone and his friends do, despite its painful obviousness. Pasolini has used Amore to embody in the extreme that condition less readily apparent in the actions of others.

Accatone's ambivalence for the material world assumes the proportions of self-disfiguration. During the riverside party where he first toys with the notion of marketing Stella, he climbs a bridge (apparently driven by pangs of remorse) with the intention of diving into the water, an act most clearly reminiscent of the opening sequence. When prevented from jumping, he runs to the water's edge and buries his face in the sand. This deliberate gesture gives him the look of a werewolf; disfigured with sand, his face is a mask of mud through which two anguished eyes protrude. Clearly, his befoulment is an act of consummate frustration directed at the sheer intractability of material existence. Unable to deal with the world creatively, Accatone finds in it only a means of blemishing himself, of negating his image.

In one dimension of the film the sundering of spirit and flesh which typifies the collective consciousness of the characters is translated into a tension between gravity and levitation, between things weighted into immobility by mass and those empowered to move. For example, the opening sequence of shots, while delineating Accatone's insistent urge for individuation, also creates a dialectical contrast between Fulvio, in motion, bearing an armful of featherlike flowers (like those in the final episode) and the Accatone crowd, seated immobile and masslike in their dark clothes.

The general theme extends to the wager Accatone makes with his friends, for it turns on his ability to defy gravity (and thus defy the concrete world) by swimming the river with a kilogram of pasta in his gut and his gold trinkets (as bystanders notice) dangling from his neck. And while he evinces the capacity to accomplish this defiance (and move), the performance becomes increasingly difficult in the course of the film. Accatone's disdain of the world seems to aggravate the vigor of its grasp upon him. Thus by the final portions of the film his wrestling with weight, specifically in the iron rings he loads as part of his job, totally depletes his energy. He collapses. The more strongly he strives to rise above the world, the greater its pull upon him. One can say with some accuracy that his activity in the final portion of the film forms one long parabola of descent. That is, not only does he die prone on the ground, but his locomotion is directed predominately downward. His itinerary to his job takes him through a series of sloped streets and he enters the office by descending a stairway. Love draws him into life, but his congenital scorn for existence thwarts his efforts to fulfill the promise of that love. While he disengages himself from a life founded on enslaving others, he remains indentured to an ideal inconsistent with a universe holistically ordered. Having metaphysically split reality, he falls into the rejected portion.

Maddelena

As I have already suggested, Pasolini uses his secondary characters rather skillfully either to magnify indistinct properties of the central figures or to shed light on the spiritual contours of society. In the failures of Maddelena, the issue of poor perception is given definite form. She reveals a total visual ineptitude and is, indeed, a perceptual cripple. When first seen, she has just been struck by a motorcycle which she failed to see. She identifies Don Salvatore by his voice, but fails to recognize him by his image when he spirits her away for a beating. In the police station, she identifies, with complete certitude, the wrong group of men as her assailants. She seems to live primarily through words and by so doing suffers the pitfalls of a word-dominated consciousness. She believes Accatone loves her because he tells her so, then informs the police of his activities, a repetition of her relations with Ciccio. Words are closely affiliated with the petit bourgeois dreams and delusions of the characters, with their efforts to place mediators between themselves and the world. Language creates the illusions of rarified polish and honor with which the Accatone crowd dress themselves, placing words, like blocks, between themselves and the reality of what they are.

Words in *Accatone*, then, are misused as tools for deceit or as abstractions with no value (the codes of honor which govern most of the males). Words become shelters for egocentricism. Thus Accatone can verbally recognize himself as a bastard while robbing his son, but, nevertheless, carry out the robbery. His friends in the spaghetti scene become easy victims of words, and with Don Salvatore words merely mask (euphemistically) a treacherous personality. Those who function in the world at all positively (such as the police in the final episode) rely upon vision, since it connects one directly to the world and to the energies erupting there. This may explain the emphasis given the detective's eyes in the last part of the movie. But the emphasis also tells us something about Accatone and explains why Pasolini sees his change as positive.

Accatone is always more visually alert than his friends, thus more sensitive to beauty and more capable of love. Stella, associated with light, is an eye-opener of sorts and, in his own way, so is Balilla (the thief). More relevant, compared with pimping, which is based upon verbal and physical domination, thievery necessitates visual alertness (which is ironically what the three men lack at the end). But within this context Accatone, by virtue of his attraction for Stella, his pursuit of light in his dream, and his vocation as a thief, has grown progressively away from verbal control (associated with polarization and the master/slave relationship) to visual relationships (associated with motion, growth, and immersion in reality). Vision in the film tends to individuate and foster love; language tends to sustain the old system with its securities and squalor. Moreover, it is not hard to see how an entire vision of the nature and generation of "exploitative" capitalism—love instincts prostituted into master/slave classes in service to profit—is contained in this picture of subproletarian life. Vision becomes a function of language, and with it human relationships are reduced to schematic codes: women are limited to the verbally imposed categories of saint or whore and become the slaves of men. Life becomes a function of abstraction and profit. In this manner, Pasolini brings together his political concerns with his sense of the nature of the medium.

Style

Stylistically, *Accatone* is surprisingly well integrated for a first film. Careful examination of almost any particular frame or sequence yields a wealth of significant detail. The editorial achievements of the opening scenes have already been mentioned. In addition to this sort of thematic editing, Pasolini is able to use his camera to reveal a variety of tensions between characters. For example, on several occasions it opens a scene, seemingly, as a slave to the dialogue only to leave the speakers to follow apparently irrelevant figures in motion. However, this action often discovers new figures who in some way introduce change or conflict in a scene.

Following Fulvio in the opening scene as he turns to leave while the conversation continues, the camera discovers Accatone's brother coming up the street. The process is repeated in a later scene when, bored with the conversation of Accatone's group, the camera begins following a child and discovers the police coming toward the group. Thus, while asserting a sense of freedom, the camera introduces a pattern of objects moving at cross-purposes, a correlative to Accatone's own self-defeating behavior.

Probably the most interesting stylistic feature of the film involves the director's use of perspective. The emphasis upon frontal shots in the earlier section of the film tends to reduce the sense of perspective in the order of the frame. When it does become visible, the vanishing point (or the point of linear convergence) usually lies outside the frame, as when Fulvio moves about in the opening sequence or when Accatone drives home to see Maddelena. When he is perched atop the bridge, a low angle shot is used which minimalizes the background and the line of the bridge.

The sense of perspective increases in the second portion of the movie (following Maddelena's beating) as Accatone begins to look more reflectively upon his own life, that is, to "gain depth." Thus we have the long scene in which Accatone follows Ascenza up a road coming directly at the retreating camera, while the lines of the roadway, with its string of light poles, converge at a vanishing point at center screen behind the protagonists. One facet of this kind of perspective is the sensation it purveys of human activity conditioned within a rigid, abstract system. It stresses a type of linear motion in a large depth of field, providing vistas of new places to go, but a sense of restriction on how to go. At the same time, the sense of perspective is a product of Accatone's growing perspective on himself.

But, of course, as Accatone's impulses are fraught with contradiction, the perspectival image has a double edge. While he is most often shown in the middle portion of the frame, moving outward from the vanishing point (with Ascenza, with Stella buying the dress, and, afterward, walking alone in the street, or coming to Fulvio's with the spaghetti), in the final episodes he moves directly into the vanishing point in what becomes a process of entrapment (going to work, wandering with the thieves, or crossing the bridge in his dream). The streets are increasingly lined with heavy masses of stone buildings, suggesting the encroachment of both the physical world he desires to escape and the "establishment" from which he seeks liberation. The dualistic perception conditioning his activity creates a "perspective trap." At film's end he leaps onto a motorcycle and rolls into the vanishing point, disappearing around a corner. He is at last shown in an aperspectival close-up which suggests both his release from the perspective trap and his subsequent death resulting from the escapist nature of his enterprise (since he is literally escaping from the police here).

Recurrent Motifs

Within the general context of the film there are several motifs worth discussing. One of the most prominent is that of the missing father; both Accatone and Stella have been abandoned, Ciccio is missing from his family, and Accatone is himself a missing father. All of this tends to suggest the condition of the world in which the action occurs. There are no ultimate guides or authorities; the individual is on his own. But unable to live with this situation, each seeks out a father figure: Maddelena a pimp, Don Salvatore a sheltering group philosophy, Ascenza her literal father, and Accatone's friends the priests who provide them with food. To remain eternally in search of a father, of course, means to remain eternally a child, which explains the presence of all the children in the film. (Accatone even kicks one after drinking with Don Salvatore.)

The quest for a father is associated with all the crossing and posturing-as-prayer that occurs. In the early frames, Accatone's companion, who addresses Fulvio, begins in a position with head bowed and hands clasped in prayer. Accatone will unconsciously make the sign of the cross before diving from the bridge and Balilla will close the film by crossing himself. The gestures are, on the one hand, merely dead rituals and, on the other hand, revelations of the immaturity and dualism of those who make them. The cross tends to embody the sense of cross-purpose in the human activity in the film.

With the motif of the rings, one can clearly see how images can develop as a process. In the opening episode Accatone proffers his ring as substance to his wager that he can swim the river. Later he will try to sell this ring. As the polarization in his perception and identity becomes aggravated, the rings become large, heavy rings of iron, dragging him down to a world whose necessities he eschews; they become images of his initial bourgeois attachment to jewelry. At the same time the ring is normally associated with marriage, but in Accatone's case, as the iron rings suggest, a marriage with life is becoming increasingly difficult. He is encircled, or "ringed," in death by the circle of police and friends around him; he weds himself to death, not life: the tragic result of his aspiration to flee the demands of necessity. The ring from which he attempts to separate himself becomes the ring of society, which stifles him in his very inability to establish a productive relationship with it.

In the last analysis, try as he will to free himself, Accatone fails really to assimilate the experiences of his life. Instead, by his rebellion against the world, he becomes weighted down by life, passing out from its gifts (as from his wine drinking) or simply failing to absorb, immerse in, and assimilate it. The pursuit of Stella, the embodiment of religious salvation, requires literally leaving behind the spaghetti at Fulvio's (physical necessity) or appropriating the world in such a way (theft) as to be self-defeating. One can infer, in light of Pasolini's own way of seeing reality, that Accatone fails in the world because he lacks the imagination to relate to it. He cannot relate creatively to what he cannot perceive as bearing inherent value. To see the world as sacred—as Pasolini feels one must—is to see it in terms of creative possibilities as well as ugliness and hardship.

The film, then, on its political side, offers a detailed vision of the factors involved in the formation of an exploitative class system, factors which begin with a failure in human relationships. Such a failure begins with the individual's fear of both his natural roots and his imaginative capabilities. Rather than engage life as a fully "synthetic" activity, Accatone and friends choose to cleave to sheltering "identities" (honor, pimphood, thiefhood) which prove to be inoperable abstractions.

3

Mamma Roma: A Son's Best Friend

ALTHOUGH *Mamma Roma* was, and continues to be, poorly received in comparison to *Accatone*, the two films have a great deal in common. Like the story of *Accatone*, *Mamma Roma* involves the self-destruction of a character who commands our sympathy as well as our scorn. As in the earlier film, prostitution is both the occupation of the protagonist and the metaphor which defines his or her spiritual failure. The idea inherent in the metaphor proclaims that the selling of oneself for money is symptomatic of a mentality which perceives oneself, others, and happiness in terms of consumer products. The moral result of this condition is revealed as a desire to withdraw from life and to substitute wholly material objects for love and the life of the spirit. Thus Ettore, the son of the protagonist, Mamma Roma, is given a petit-bourgeois job and the straightjacket pretensions of a refined petit bourgeois existence rather than a much needed injection of honesty which could impel him toward spiritual growth. While *Accatone* embodied these issues in a manner largely poetic and metaphysical, *Mamma Roma* handles them much more explicitly, even more problematically.[1]

As in *Accatone*, the substitution of material for emotional values has a contradictory twist to it. In seeking fulfillment in life, both Mamma Roma and Accatone try to withdraw into a refined, materialistic lifestyle in which they can actually shrink from the crude reality of physical life and, indeed, try to pretend that it does not exist. Both seek a haven from humiliating realities: Mamma Roma refuses to face Ettore with the truth about her past (to preserve her sense of respectability) and Accatone considers turning his beloved Stella into a prostitute (to avoid working). Disdaining the commonality of life, both place themselves above the morality they expect to find in others. In shrinking from the possibility of failure, both try to disown responsibility for their lives, ignoring the inexorable consequences of their exploitation or deceit upon their own destinies.

49

Mama Roma: *Ettore Garofolo in his world of circular forms, pawning Mama's phonograph record.*

In both films, "dualism," the fracturing of the holistic nature of the world into irreconcilable opposites of spirit and flesh, plays a major role. In failing to keep faith with the life of the world, each character suffers a personality split, maintaining two incompatible identities. Thus, while Accatone, at various times, is either the "spiritual" Vittorio or the pimp Accatone, Mamma Roma is either the vulgar prostitute/con artist by night or the respectable petit bourgeois merchant by day, seeking the guiding light of the parish priest in regulating her life. Founded on such chaos, her efforts to create a new life for herself (to be fulfilled largely through Ettore) engender only more chaos. In its most radical state, her life becomes reduced to the pursuit of static, vague ideals of success through which she struggles to wed herself to life, much as Accatone tries to do with the overidealized Stella.

The choice of the "wedding metaphor" to describe the condition of wholeness sought for but eternally unrealized by Mamma Roma is particularly appropriate since the film opens upon a wedding, or more precisely, the defilement of a wedding reception. We are shown a group of swine, grunting and squealing, being driven into the reception room. A moment later, the swineherd is revealed to be the heroine, Mamma Roma. By her brazen domination of the conversation, her bawdy songs (which are at best barrenly titillating), and her totally self-centered behavior, she appears to be nothing less than the soul of vulgarity. Her good spirits, using the wedding as an excuse, bubble into an infantile animality. Her festive mood seems as much self-advertisement as celebration: a personality seeking the confirmation of its existence in the approbation of an audience. It no doubt satisfies her that, despite her separate lives, she is never addressed by a personal name, but always identified—even by herself in dreams—by the public nickname "Mamma Roma." Her consciousness has no personal center.

If Mamma Roma's behavior seems overly coarse, the entire reception is no less a defilement of sorts, for it is set up pictorially to closely resemble Leonardo's painting "The Last Supper." In place of Christ and his disciples, Pasolini places Carmine, a pimp and blackmailer, and a host of confidence men and prostitutes. The deliberate resemblance of the scene to the painting, coupled with the extreme vulgarity and materialistic orientation of the guests, intimates not the wholeness of their consciousness but a polarity in sensibility in which the life of the spirit and the life of the flesh are already dissociating or at best conjoined unharmoniously. Or, perhaps more simply, by their conversion of "The Last Supper" into a pigsty, the wedding group betrays its aesthetic callousness and insensibility to the presence of creative spirit in the world. By comparison with the ideal spiritual figures of Leonardo, they prove themselves ideally crass and uncompassionate. Thus, despite the presence in the scene of both spiritual and materialistic sides of reality, one is left more with a feeling of their severance than union, of the absence, really, of the spiritual in the lives of the main characters.

While these metaphysical issues condition the nature of the tragedy and serve to explain it, what compels our attention is Mamma Roma's evasion and final confrontation of the complicity of her values in the destruction of her life. This drama, structured by her petit bourgeois materialism and her tendency to live through other people, finds its focus in her relationship with Ettore. Their mutual failure in communion is shaped by the effort of the mother to redeem her life through converting Ettore into an image of her own values of refinement and conformity. As he is modeled to fulfill this ideal of a petit bourgeois lifestyle, he is reduced to being a consumer product and an extension of her ego, a symbol of her ability to conform. And since such conformity is an act of bad faith in oneself, Ettore becomes a substitute for the spiritual growth she has abjured.

Ettore's role as a substitute is built simultaneously on various levels of the film. For example, on a rather Freudian plane, there are strong suggestions that Ettore has become a replacement to his mother for her missing husband, almost a surrogate lover. At times, especially in the early scenes of the movie, she seems to flirt with him. Thus, in the scene in which Mamma Roma introduces Ettore to their new dwelling, she entices him into a dance that concludes with her falling on top of him. Similarly, with complete innocence, she relates a previous night's dream in which she heard the voice of her husband calling to her on a mountain plateau (he refers to her as "Mamma Roma"). But when she looks after the source of the call, she finds Ettore instead.

But this dimension of his surrogate function is clearly unconscious and not pursued by the film. On a more conscious level, Mamma Roma uses her son to help compensate for her own sense of social inferiority. In part, what she worships in him is the possibility of her own attainment of a bourgeois life-style. He must wear refined clothes, attend a nice church, and not soil himself in a job that smacks of real work. Her obsession with settling Ettore in a proper job, as a waiter in a successful restaurant, becomes the nucleus of her destruction. Pasolini constructs the total fabric of this situation very carefully. First he provides us a clear touchstone (in the figure of a priest) by which to measure her moral delinquency. Since Ettore, being weak-willed, lazy, and uncognizant of responsibility, has neither learned a trade nor been receptive to a general education, the priest advises Mamma Roma to either place him in a trade school or caution him to accept a laborer's job which the priest will be able to secure for him. When she rejects this suggestion indignantly, he questions her further as to her own means and advises her, upon learning the truth, that she give up her false pride in herself and Ettore's work, educate him bit by bit to the truth, and approach life with more humility. Although she seems moved by the speech, she largely ignores it, for although she wants Ettore to be employed, she cannot bear the idea of his holding a blue collar job. More understandably, she cannot face Ettore with the truth of her life for fear of being rejected by him. But of course, as the priest suggests, continued deceit only makes this end more probable.

Although Mamma Roma has been exposed to a clear enough analysis of her situation, she persists in her original obsession. Having identified the proprietor of a successful restaurant in her church congregation (her real reason for attending Mass), she sets in motion a plan to ingratiate herself with him and thus win the desired job for Ettore. The man has already refused the priest's request to employ this prodigal son on the grounds that he is already fully staffed. To leap this hurdle, Mamma Roma weaves a combination confidence scheme and blackmail operation with the aid of her former colleague Biancofiore and a friend, Zacaria. They lure the proprietor into a tryst with Biancofiore which is interrupted by an outraged Zacaria claiming to be the girl's brother. He draws a knife, but Mamma Roma appears miraculously and intervenes. The proprietor escapes with only the loss of his wallet and some vague innuendos that they may inform his wife or make the incident public. He is glad to escape with Mamma Roma, who wastes no time in pressuring him to employ Ettore.

The events of this scene are given a sharply ironic twist by the fact that even as she perpetrates her blackmail scheme, Mamma Roma is herself being blackmailed by Carmine. The insinuation of the film suggests that he is her former pimp; he now demands money from her, on pain of disclosing her life to Ettore, in order to invest in a meat-selling venture—i.e., like everyone else, to establish himself in a quasi-capitalistic position.

The allegorical implications in the situation are hard to ignore: Mamma Roma, as her name suggests, represents the misguided Italian mentality, coarsened by an exploitative capitalism, yet subscribing to largely the same values as her exploiter. Fortunately, the dramatic immediacy of the story transcends its allegorical trajectory and we find ourselves involved ambivalently in the emotional situation of Mamma Roma: condemning her on the one hand for her vanity and deceit, sympathizing with her on the other as she is throttled by a miscreant worse than herself. She seems more victim than victimizer.

The final twist in this reflexive blackmail situation is pronounced when Ettore learns the truth (to what degree Carmine is capable of truth) about his mother. Swollen with self-pity, he determines to even himself with his mother and the world by becoming the proper progeny of a soiled mother: a thief. Like the swindle wrought by his mother, the scheme contrived by him and his friends is a confidence game in which they will enter a hospital as visitors (and patients) in order to gain access to whatever they can steal. Clearly, in the progress of the film, one act of bad faith tends to engender only similar acts.

In addition to the complications of the plot, our response to Mamma Roma is modified by another set of conditioning factors: the gallery of personalities which surrounds her. With the exception of the priest who provides her with semiuseful advice, Mamma Roma's friends are less savory than she. Carmine, for example, although technically no more a swindler, is much colder and calculating, capable of no compassion and exhibiting no capacity to feel joy or love. In his final confrontation with her, he is rendered the more egotistical of the two. His speech, in fact, in which he claims to have raised Mamma Roma from the gutter, fathering his own ruin by acting as pimp for her, is uttered almost word for word by Accatone to Maddelena in the earlier film. The character, of course, is played by the same person (Franco Citti). In comparison to Carmine, Mamma Roma is at least ingenious in her schemes and perceptive enough to choose victims who can afford a fleecing.

In measuring her against her other acquaintances, one feels she once again emerges superior. For while all ply roughly the same trade, she is at least awakened to the possibility of living in a less barbarous manner; she feels a pressure to grow in some direction.

Even Ettore, given his debilitating parental influence, comes off as morally inferior to his mother. With the exception of his romantic response to Bruna, he sleepwalks through most of the movie with an incredible passivity and lack of awareness about the necessities of life. His condition, a pathetic disaffection from reality, may have been fostered by his mother, but it cannot be wholly attributed to her. He is lost in a fantasy life, a condition aptly depicted in his initial appearance—slumped and immobile in the chair of a merry-go-round, obscured by the seat as though deliberately hiding. Rows of airy balloons, which line the amusement park, supplement the sense of detachment and unreality which surrounds him.

On those occasions when Ettore does engage in enough activity to suggest he is alive, his deeds have a pronounced negative inflection. Hence his first individualizing act is the theft of a phonograph record from his mother which he pawns to buy a trinket for Bruna. In the spirit of irony which infests the film, Pasolini has the girl immediately ask Ettore if he has a job or an education. He dismisses both questions cavalierly. In the denouement of the film, in a futile attempt to assert an identity, Ettore becomes a petty thief, still merely rebelling against his mother. With a rather unwarranted sense of indignity, he passes her stall in the marketplace without deigning to acknowledge her existence.

His actions (after being enlightened about his mother) remain patterned on an adolescent sense of adulthood as a state of cynical toughness. However, his pretensions are quickly stripped away when he is incarcerated by the police. Tied to a table, he dies calling for his mother, a scene at once compelling yet revelatory of his bondage to a state of perpetual childhood.

The emphatic sense of immobility stressed in this scene (as well as that of the concluding one in which Mamma Roma collapses in her apartment) discloses a cinematic aspect to the moral condition of the characters. In a significant sense, the film can be seen as a study in false change, therefore, false motion. The immobilization of Ettore at the film's end is an epiphany of his inability to grow. The seeming changes in his personality are rather illusory. The illusion of change is, of course, an even more prominent feature of his mother's life, she who expressed the desire to "start life over from zero." But instead of initiating any real change in her life, she substitutes one form of prostitution (literal) for another (a petit bourgeois value system). One aspect of this false change in the film is the substitution of the mechanical for the organic. Thus Mamma Roma supplants the fledgling introduction to life Ettore needs with the gift of a motorcycle. The bike serves, of course, as a status symbol as well as a mechanical substitute for the fertility each lacks in his or her emotional life.

Ettore's motorcycle is really just one of a number of objects used as substitutes, each associated with nondirectional, circular motion. First, of course, is the merry-go-round Ettore rides in his first appearance; in the context of false change, it is essentially a wheel going nowhere. The merry-go-round is succeeded by the phonograph record, another self-circling disk, to which mother and son dance, wheeling around each other. The record, it may be suggested, yields to the con game itself, whose moral shape is quite clearly circular by its use of fraud to engender an "honest" life: it provides the illusion of advancement without the substance. The motorcycle more or less fulfills this parade of circular forms, constructed as it is upon two wheels. Although it is intended as transportation to work, Ettore never uses it as such. It remains a detached mechanical symbol, unintegrated into the practical needs of his life.

Just as the motorbike is never used to "go anywhere" (other than one brief joyride), so none of the characters ever goes anywhere by the end of the film. The more Mamma Roma pursues her new life, the more she relies on the cronies of her old life (Biancofiore, for instance)—or the more they return of their own will to haunt her. Ettore fares no better; he ends as he began, immobilized and constricted by his inability to assume responsibility for himself. Carmine is similarly, indeed even more, unregenerate at film's end, having used Mamma Roma as the scapegoat for his prodigality.

The sense of false change important to the moral center of the film is with varying success captured by *Mamma Roma*'s stylistic peculiarities. Particularly noticeable are the several extremely long tracking shots in the night scenes. By placing the characters against a dark background, then herding them toward a camera which retreats with their advance, Pasolini consigns their movement to a limbo of sorts: they walk as though on a treadmill, not seeming to advance. This use of frontal shots is successfully applied to the motorcycle ride as well. (On the other hand, the camera tends to follow Mamma Roma from behind on those occasions when she enters her new apartment complex, with an effect that does not vitiate her sense of motion, but creates the impression of entering a restricted prison cell.)

The sense of false change is further supported by the choice of mise-en-scène, the Roman ruins not far from Cinecitta. The characters walk through broken columns and useless aquaducts, perpetually caught up in a dead past from which they cannot free themselves.

Mamma Roma provides an excellent example of how Pasolini's Marxist sympathies cannot be taken loosely and applied to his films as an interpretative index. The problems of the characters do not arise simply from the social system, nor can they be solved by it. Their failures remain matters of the individual soul, which cradles, in its sleeping capacity to love, its own salvation. Their failures arise from the seat of human loneliness which seeks refuge in social conformity and the consensus reality of material values.

Mamma Roma is, for most viewers, not as primally powerful as *Accatone*, whose neo-realist style is charged with a greater sense of mystery and poetry. Nevertheless, it is a rather underrated film. Its structure, its dramatic conflicts, and its exploitation of images are carefully developed and harmonized. They contain dimensions which may well elude a viewer on a single screening. The film is neither a failure nor an aberration in Pasolini's development. It fits coherently into his total canon, yet stands on its own strengths as good film.

The Gospel According to St. Matthew: *(top) Christ's followers in their typical "S" formation witness the miracle of loaves and fishes; (bottom) Enrique Irazoqui as Jesus shouldering his cross*

4

The Gospel According to Matthew:
Meta-Cinema and Epical Vision

THE GOSPEL ACCORDING TO MATTHEW is a difficult film for many people, in part, because it seems completely guileless and open. Some critics have attempted to torture it into being a Marxist declaration,[1] but not only has Pasolini played down the film's Marxist elements, a close scrutiny reveals it to be, if anything, anti-ideological: "My film is a reaction against the conformity of Marxism. The mystery of life and of death and of suffering—and particularly of religion—is something which Marxists do not want to consider."[2] In the context of the previous two feature films, *Gospel* brings to a provisional resolution his concerns with holistic consciousness, an immanent potential in each man, smothered by his hunger for material supremacy. Pasolini's interest lies less in transforming the story of Christ into a political allegory than in "re-consecrating" it.[3] Thus, at the heart of the film lies the issue of visual connection with the world: "But internally nothing I've ever done has been more fitted to me myself than *The Gospel* . . . my tendency always to see something sacred and mythic in everything, even the most humdrum, simple and banal objects and events."[4]

Pasolini's concerns with religious consciousness were elaborated in an interview in *Film Culture* shortly after finishing this film. Speaking in regard to *The Hawks and the Sparrows*, he suggested that his general concerns at this period of his career bear largely upon the conflict of two modes of perception, rational and imaginative.[5] The latter of these involves, particularly, a sensitivity to the irrational and mysterious dimensions of life, a sensitivity which results in an experience of the world's wholeness, the interpenetration of spirit and flesh. The rationalist mode, by virtue of its orientation toward factual truth, is useful but limited; it cannot confront life as a mystery. By its reduction of experience to measurable forms of knowledge, it cannot comprehend the presence of dynamic spirit as a creative suprarational force in the world. Part of

59

the particular dynamic of *The Gospel According to Matthew* emerges from the interaction of these two modes, the former being embodied in Christ and the latter typifying the limited and, hence, fallen vision of the world he enters.

One question which inevitably arises in discussing the film is the degree to which its subject matter and impact are purely derived from the Book of Matthew. The film does indeed follow the tenor of the book, but to see it as only a visual rendering of (or visual aid to) its source is to misperceive it. First, there is a great deal in Matthew omitted in the film: the healing of Peter's mother-in-law, the casting of spirits into the swine, and much of chapter 9. Moreover, the film does not rigidly follow the order of Matthew; the disciples are collected in one fell swoop in the film, the events with the Pharisees are altered (i.e., the grain field episode), and many scenes have been invented: Phillip and Bartholomew running on the beach, the casual passing of the scribes at Jesus' baptism, an episode in which Judas buys food as Jesus speaks, and much of the dance of Salome. In other words, Matthew's gospel has been molded just enough to endow it with a new narrative emphasis.

Pasolini's narrative tends to focus upon the growth of Christ, whereas much more of Matthew is taken up specifically with Christ's sermonizing. What we see in the Pasolini version is a movement from Jesus as infant, to his awakening sense of his identity, to the actualization of his mission, to his trials and the final realization of his destiny. As such, it shares with *Accatone* the concern with individuation—individual self-realization—but it also transfers this concern to the stylistic nature of the film itself as a "meta-theme." That is, if it is the individual's image which is of importance, then the value of the film must be in some sense dictated by the nature of the image rather than by obvious editorial control. The direction of the story must emanate from inside-out rather than outside-in; the style must operate as a function of the protagonist. The protagonist is to "redeem" the film rather than be redeemed by it, as Accatone partially was (in Pasolini's original conception).

Style

Because it is in Pasolini's treatment of the subject rather than his creation of original narrative that his creative work lies, the relationship of the protagonist to the style, the visual rendering of the story, must be a central feature of any discussion of the film.

Pasolini began shooting the film in the manner he had used with *Accatone*, employing many direct frontal shots and a short-length focal lens which can sculpture the character's features.[6] He seems to have felt this "sacramental" style was "gilding the lily," and switched to a variety of other techniques, including zoom shots, a hand-held camera, various length lenses—all of which compel the viewer into an awareness of his "spectatorhood" and make him feel that even the camera is more a spectator than a creator. The film purveys the flavor of a documentary, which allows the subject a natural dominance. Because the religious qualities of the film must emerge from within its context, not through the obvious imposition of style from without, the film has a very existential dimension to it: whatever essence exists (i.e., ideas, values), emerges from the nature of Christ's existence. He becomes a self-sufficient force as a person and a film image.

The film's stylistic features are wrought as though dictated by the subject, and consequently they quite naturally emphasize Christ's uniqueness, particularly his magnetic power as an image and his radiance as a center of love. The extended use of the zoom shot, by its nature of moving from the general to the particular, becomes a cinematic statement of individuation. It singles out the individual from the mass, but more importantly it suggests the compelling attraction and power of the figure toward whom it is drawn. It is precisely the kind of stylistic feature which, because it emanates from the nature of its subject, draws one to speak of style being a function of content rather than vice versa. There are approximately twenty occurrences of this shot in the film, beginning with Joseph's dream in the first episode to Christ's resurrected pose at the end.

The use of the zoom shot creates a second important quality: the flattening of space. On the one hand, it tends to blur the background, thus drawing attention to the central image, and on the other, it reduces the sense of perspective in the frame. This technique does not imply the superficiality of Christ; rather, by eliminating perspective, it eliminates the artificial or "rational" sense of space and frame composition by which objects may appear geometrically organized. The perspectival frames tend to occur in moments of rational dominance in the film, as in an early scene in which a skeptical Joseph departs into a rigid one-point perspective frame. The dissolution of the perspectival frame becomes the stylistic equivalent to the triumph of mystery and love over reason in the film.

The concern with the value of the individual is also reflected in the massive number of close-ups in the film. However, as opposed to *Accatone*, the concern with the individual in *The Gospel* is more for his inherent and unique mystery than his moral individuation. At certain points the film becomes a collage of these close-ups, most apparently in Jesus' long sermons to his disciples and in the slaughter of the innocents by Herod's army. Similarly, the opening of the film proper is composed of a series of reverse-angle close-ups of Mary and Joseph, thus stating from the outset the concern for the inpenetrable mystery of the human face. If nothing else, the film leaves one with a sense of the infinite possibilities of man's image, from the lean anxiety of the chief Pharisee to the anguish of Judas, Mary, and Peter, each in his different way.

But, as I have said, the film, by its subject matter and relationship to Pasolini's other films, is concerned with the relationship of spirit and flesh. While the previous films portrayed people who failed to perceive the potential unity of the two, *The Gospel According to Matthew* is concerned with a figure in whom these realities appear united, at least in the eyes of his followers: "I followed the Christ of Matthew: that is, a figure who was man and God at the same time."[7]

Because the narrative material itself evokes a vision of unification and harmony (despite the conflict of rational and imaginative perception), there is a general sense of balance in the lighting, brilliant but low-contrast photography (or fill lighting) which makes manifest the latent integration of polarized value (spirit/flesh) rather than its radical disjunction, as in *Accatone* or *Mamma Roma*. The dominant quality of the images is not a light/dark contrast (which does exist at points) but a luminous grey fusion.

This sense of unified poles has to some degree been actualized in the image of Jesus, particularly in the scene in which he begins his mission while passing some laborers in a grain field. Draped about his head is a dark shawl in a rather effeminate manner, reminding one of the opening shots of Mary. The tails of the shawl trail from each side like those of a woman's scarf. Yet underneath this feminine pose, Christ moves in an aggressive manner, addressing his future disciples with masculine authority and evangelical fire.

In accordance with his self-integration and magnetism, Christ tends to control the camera motion in a leader-follower relationship. As a result, he is often viewed moving with his back to the camera, as though drawing it magnetically. Certainly the zoom shots emphasize this relationship. His potency as an image becomes the "perceived" creative force within the film, more than the ostensible editorial control of the camera or director. This existential relationship of image to camera becomes an inherent statement of Christ's powers of self-liberation, consummated in his resurrection: he waits outside the frame for the camera while it gropes from the empty tomb leftward, following the crowd to his presence. Meta-cinematically, then, Christ's story is a story of Pasolini's liberation of the image itself, as an aesthetic phenomenon, from any particular set of ideological premises that would restrict its value to a rational meaning and control. And herein we come to one of the primary processes in the film, the transcendence of rational vision.

The Narrative Process

Pasolini chooses to begin the film's narrative with a confrontation between Joseph and Mary which contains at its heart a confrontation between rational and imaginative perception. A close-up of Mary, a dark-skinned girl with soft features and an expression of solemnity, is followed by a reverse-angle close-up of a frowning Joseph. He is skeptical and uncomprehending of the miraculous event at hand. He departs and we see him from behind, enclosed, so to speak, in the rigid perspectival lines of the road formed by its stone walls.

The extreme presence of abstract organization within the frame operates as a visual extension of the predominantly rational set of assumptions under which Joseph is laboring. He passes some small children and sits in the corner of a rock and sleeps. It is here at this extreme enclosure that he experiences a liberating vision: an ambisexual angel appears, explains the situation, and urges him to return to Mary. The angel's presence is first outside the frame and must be discovered by the camera. Hence, in this scene we have a model for the process of the film-entire: a displacement of rational perception by epical vision, an awakening to immanent divinity.

The story of Herod which follows extends the definition of rationalist perception to include paranoia and obsession with power. Herod's court is dominated by the figure of the rigid square, along whose borders stand scribes and lackeys in rigid file. The dominance of worldly control and abstraction is abundantly evident. Herod's world, like that of all those dominated by rationalistic perception, is a "head" world, a fact emphasized by the ponderous conelike miters of the court scribes. Their visual top-heaviness purveys an almost synesthetic feeling of disequilibrium to the viewer, suggesting the imbalance of the priests' perceptual modality. Herod's death scene is appropriately concluded with the binding of his head with rags by three old women.

While Herod's perception, sustained only by his egoconsciousness, results in paranoiac slaughter—significantly a slaughter of the inno-

cent—the vision of Joseph and Mary continues to be informed by suprarational power, and, led by an angel, they escape the impending havoc. Their motion toward a center of love and visual energy is, again, a model of the moral process purveyed in theme and style.

The slaughter of the innocents is enhanced by at least two interesting stylistic features. First is the length of time the camera devotes to the face of each soldier. The concern for individuality is underscored by the fact that each soldier wears a radically different helmet from those of his comrades. The attention applied to head gear again suggests the essentially rationalist "head" approach to life (as opposed to an integral spiritual approach) which characterizes Christ's opponents.

In addition, the attack of the soldiers results in a pattern of frame composition which will be repeated on several occasions in association with innocence and imagination. The first shots of the attack are relatively long shots which allow us to study the movement of the victims. Initially, their attempts at escape take a definable form of an S curve, in one shot moving upward, in another downward. One's initial response, because of the serpentine quality of the curve, is to associate it with Satan, but the structure does not seem to be working by such exterior reference. Rather, its curvilinear form provides a geometrical contrast to the unnatural rectilinear figures which prevail in the world of the rationalists. Several shots later, as the camera approaches the baptism of Jesus from an extreme long shot, the S structure is again prominent, this time formed by the river itself, associating it with the forms of nature. In addition to providing the S composition, the water is a new motif in the film. Its emergence in correlation to the first appearance of Christ as a man promotes a sense of the imminent infusion of life and spirit into a spiritually dry world. Water tends to be associated with Christ, as in the water-walking episode and several scenes preceding his trial. It appears at the suicide of Judas. A waterfall occupies a spot in the far background left as Judas ties his rope to a branch; the distance between the two suggests the spiritual distance of Judas from Jesus.

The S composition is prominent again as Christ enters Capernaum; it appears in a following scene in the city in which he stands atop a rampart while his followers, in an S formation, listen on the steps below, and most explicitly in a long shot of Christ entering Jerusalem on the donkey. This shot is repeated moments later from a slightly different angle.

Jesus' baptism scene again contains a structural tension between epical and rationalist perception; skeptical Pharisees pass by the epochal event oblivious to the miracle of the dove and God's voice. The opposition of holistic to materialistic value underlies the next episode in the film, Satan's temptation of Christ. The thick-lipped, curly-haired, "hard"-featured Satan is strongly carnal in his appearance. Moreover, his dissociated nature is manifested visually by focusing on that part of Satan most associated with earth, his feet, then cutting to his head, severing the two on the screen. By contrast Pasolini's vision of Christ in this scene, by virtue of the latter's physical strength and resolution, seems not so much that of a Jesus lapsing into a spiritual netherworld but of a man of unified spirit and flesh. (There is, admittedly, a great deal of ambiguity in Christ's manner, for while he must [in the film] be a figure of this world, his teachings, taken straightforwardly from Matthew, often speak of a heaven removed from earth. Moreover, he often seems emotionally "hard" in contrast to his message of love.)

There now follow two shots of John the Baptist, a medium frontal shot and a close-up, which tend to communicate or embody our own sense of anticipation in regard to Jesus. But more than that, they reveal John's own groping attempt to accept the divine nature of Jesus (he will later send messengers asking if Jesus is the Christ). We may infer that John is trapped between the two modes of perception in the film, and his face, accordingly, is shot half-lighted, one side dark, the other side light. His condition is thus a foil to Christ's fusion of opposites and, appropriately, the film cuts from John's face to the figure of the young Jesus cloaked in his feminine shawl, initiating his mission in the world. The abundance of rear-angle footage here again manifests Christ's power for leading the camera, a sense of magnetism paralleled in the manner by which he attracts Peter, Bartholomew, and his other disciples. Jesus leads his brood away in a series of alternating long shots and close-ups, in most cases with his back to the camera as a gesture of his compelling power. Interestingly, the general movement in this scene is downward and thus "into the world," rather than upward toward heaven. It embodies Pasolini's own sense of purpose to reconsecrate reality.

Following the general model established in the opening episode (movement toward vision), the gathering of the disciples flows naturally into a scene of Christ's miracles (the healing of the insane and the curing of a leper), each of which has been deliberately relocated from its position in Matthew. And the sequence which follows recapitulates this process. From a close-up of the eyes of the healed leper (which suggests strongly the visual suprarational nature of epical perception) we move to some extreme long shots, preludes to the Sermon on the Mount. This scene, as suggested earlier, is a cinematic apotheosis of the human face. This long verbal—"rationalist"—appeal by Christ concludes in a supra-rationalist miracle: the healing of a cripple in the presence of four Pharisees. The events, though taken from Matthew, have been resynthesized by Pasolini to carry out his narrative process. The episode again ends with a close-up of the eyes of the healed man, strongly associating the transformative power of Christ with the opening of the eye, the liberation of vision from its crippled state of fallen rationalist perception to the awareness of love. By contrast, Judas is singled out purchasing food in this episode, while the miraculous activity pours forth. The holistic and materialistic modes of perception are clearly distinguished.

Christ moves away, again, with his back to the camera. We see him preaching to a group of people, his disciples complaining about the lack of food, and, finally, the miracle of the loaves. Harmonic low-contrast photography is evident here, endowing the frame with a sense of immanent spirit. Christ at times seems to be an apparition of diffuse light, and the images, in general, attain a luminescence absent in the earlier films, a perceivable sense of harmony in keeping with the director's concerns.

Christ now accomplishes his feat of walking on water (the use of the zoom shot again suggesting his magnetism) and begins his journey to Capernaum. His activity is cross-cut with the dance of Salome. In the latter scenes we may note the enclosure of the figures in a square court, as opposed to the sense of openness present in the frames of Christ. The one world appears controlled and immobile, while the other (that of Christ) is rendered open and fluid. In Capernaum Christ preaches from a building top while below him on the steps his listeners group themselves in the familiar curvilinear *S* shape. Christ rejects his mother's claim to a binding relationship in this scene, an event which prompted one critic, at least, to conclude that Pasolini was portraying Christ as a homosexual.[8] This particular event, however, as with the fact of Christ's all-male disciples, is drawn straight from Matthew and tends to manifest his increasing sense of purpose rather than his sexual predilections. As suggested earlier, the occasionally feminine appearance of Christ probably implies his fusion of possibilities rather than his sexual status.

The positioning of Christ atop the building, followed by his descent to the people in Capernaum, forms a model of his activity in the remainder of the film. He repeats this process in Jerusalem, by necessity in his crucifixion when he returns to earth. Given Pasolini's concerns, the action may be seen as an analogue to the merger of the spiritual (or heavenly) with the physical (or earthly) dimensions of reality embodied in Christ.

After scenes involving Christ's moving among the people and his reprimand to a bourgeois would-be follower, the film returns to the dance of Salome. The scene has a pronounced eery quality, created in part by the cutting from long shots to close-ups and in part by the flute music which accompanies the dance. The girl is, of course, a pawn of her mother and the placing of her episode in close proximity to Christ's own separation from Mary is probably no accident. If Christ's activity forms a model of growth, that process involves a movement beyond authoritarian figures, parental or materialistic, toward self-sufficiency. At any rate, Salome wins favor for her mother, and their combined request is for the head of John. While the episode is drawn directly from Matthew, one cannot help suggesting how well the decapitation works with the general head, or mind, control obsession of the rationalists in the film. We subsequently witness this decapitation performed, significantly, by the same actor who played Don Salvatore in *Accatone*, Umberto Bevilaqua. If Pasolini wanted a figure who suggests the separation of mind and body, he made an appropriate (if esoteric) selection. However, it is perfectly consistent with his theories of an actor representing only what he "is."[9]

The remainder of the movie deals with the consummation of Christ's role as a religious revolutionary. He enters Jerusalem, is tried, crucified, and resurrected. Stylistically, we see most of the elements previously mentioned. His entrance to the city is marked by the formation of his followers in S or reverse S curves. His trial, by contrast, is held in a rectilinear court. There is also great emphasis placed on the framed or self-limited vision of the Pharisees through their repeated placement in window or door frames (e.g., prior to their initial verbal gambit with Christ); Judas is also shown framed in a black window shortly before his betrayal. The pattern of elevation and descent is repeated and the zoom shot is prominent.

At the trial of Christ, however, a new stylistic feature is introduced: the hand-held camera. Instead of viewing the trial through a series of close-ups and medium shots, we are placed on the fringe of the crowd, looking over shoulders and around heads. The effect is startling, for it identifies us briefly with the crowd, most of whom are confused about the nature of what they see. The result, surprisingly, is to endow the proceedings with a greater epic dimension than they might have attained through conventional (or *Accatone* style) shooting. One's sense of curiosity and wonder is aroused as he is engaged by the technique in the process of trying to see, a primal concern of the film. The technique is effective precisely because it is not overused. Appropriately, the camera moves in for a close-up of Peter's eyes prior to his disavowal of discipleship.

In the following episode we witness the awakening of guilt in Judas, his return of the money, and his subsequent suicide. The shape of his "hanging tree," a large Y, suggests the divergence and splitting of his own conscience as opposed to the unifying vision of Christ.

Christ's death confirms his physical and spiritual nature. He is shown suffering intensely from the physical pain of the nails and the slow process of crucifixion. Mary is also singled out by Pasolini during this sequence, her own sufferings conveying the limitations of human imagination in the face of mortality. But the film ends not with death but rebirth; mortality, as in the Christian vision, is defeated and transformed. The shooting of this is done by identifying the camera with the mourners who come to the tomb to place flowers. The rock is rolled back and in place of Christ an angel appears professing the resurrection. The camera now moves leftward, where it discovers Jesus, and the film ends with the camera zooming in on the image of Christ, testifying to his magnetic power as both divine figure and cinematic image.

For Pasolini, *The Gospel According to Matthew* becomes the foremost expression of his own way of seeing the world: epical, holistic, and imaginative. And, in a certain sense, the film portrays a liberation of the cinematic image as an autonomous power, a power which, if considered a form of language, must be seen as being unconditional by the laws of verbal communication.[10] Christ's particular relationship to the camera in this film, his sense of "creating" its visual space rather than being defined by the frame in a manner analogous to a voice-over narration, embodies the tension of Pasolini's theoretical concerns. If Christ ends up within the camera frame, it is not a frame which has contained him but one which his activity has defined. Whether in following, questing, or zooming in upon Christ, the camera has been used as a reactor to rather than creator of Christ's presence. As opposed to the action of Accatone, whose behavior serves only to invoke the confining frames of society and his own perception, Christ tends to capture the frame and assimilate it, rather than be captured and controlled by it. Speaking speculatively in line with Pasolini's own pronouncements, one can say that through

Christ Pasolini transfers the generative core of the cinema from the literary techniques of editorial dominance to the image itself. Something of this is perhaps implied in his statement, "In *Gospel*, I completely liberated that religious element of *Accatone* which was implicit, which was in the style!"[11] While Accatone was redeemed in part externally through the style, Christ represents the internal manifestation of that power, and transition from one to the other makes clear the transition in Pasolini's own imagination. In *The Gospel According to Matthew* he discovers and realizes a vision of personal redemption, lost since the rehabilitation of Tommaso in *A Violent Life*. But while Tommaso could be saved through the intervention of an abstract, *external* social system, the Communist Party, the Christ of Pasolini's film is the possibility of every man's redemption through his own spiritual center.

5

The Hawks and the Sparrows: Eating Crow

IN MOVING FROM *The Gospel According to Matthew* to *The Hawks and the Sparrows*, Pasolini made a film in which the latent relationship between Christianity and Marxism (mystery and reason) was rendered more obvious. The basic plot of the film involves the conversations between Toto, a middle-aged man, Ninetto, his son, and a crow from "The Land of Ideology" as the three travel along a road in the Italy of the 1960s. Because of the identification of the crow as a Marxist intellectual, the viewer is ready to assume the primary freight of the film to be definably ideological (Marxist), and undeniably the film raises such issues as private property, hunger, the need for historical consciousness, and the exploitation of one class by another.

Yet the more one attempts to pin down the political message of the film, the more elusive it becomes. In his discussion of the film with John Bragin, Pasolini talks more about the limitations of Marxist ideology than he does its veracity.[1] In his prefatory discussion in the screenplay of *The Hawks and the Sparrows*, he dwells exclusively upon the nature of cinematic "language" and its autonomy from verbal language: "One always referred to this (at least in Italy) as a 'language' analogous to the written-spoken language (of literature, the theatre, etc.), and even that which is visual in it is only viewed by analogy with the figurative arts. All cinematographic examination is, therefore, erroneous at its outset because of this statute of linguistic calque."[2] In the 1969 "Pesaro Papers," Pasolini suggests that cinematic language is a language of action (motion and gesture) rather than of meaning (it is "non-symbolic" and self-referential).[3] Other comments made in interviews and essays from the period suggest a growing interest on Pasolini's part in a "process" view of life and in the nature of change.[4]

The establishment of the narrative in *The Hawks and the Sparrows* "on the road" clearly advances change and process as the central con-

73

ditions of life to be explored in the film. In regard to this there are three
dimensions of the film, or three facets of change, which can be singled
out for discussion: a linguistic dimension in which the relationship of the
film medium to life is explored; a personal drama between Toto and
Nino which becomes metaphysical; and a political or social aspect of
change dealing with the passing of neo-realism as a unitive cultural
ethos. From whichever angle of vision one approaches the film, it is significant that change itself always remains a mystery, never wholly
explained in terms of Marxist dialectic. The driving force of process in
the film is, in the Crow's own words, "religion." Allowing the Crow a
certain accuracy in this observation, especially in regard to Pasolini's use
of the word to denote a state of mind rather than an institution, the issue
at stake is a creative energy which seeks and finds expression in each of
the three levels of the film in terms of growth and assimilation.

The Story of the Medium

The manner by which the linguistic concerns of the film are integrated into the narrative is revealed in the substory (narrated by the
Crow) of Ninetto and Ciccilo. In this story Nino and Toto, the protagonists of the film, are transformed into monks of the order of St. Francis,
charged with evangelizing the birds (an unremote metaphor of Pasolini's
own quasi-Marxist proselytizing). As part of the mission they are told to
select two species from "bird-dom" who represent different classes.
They comply with the order by choosing the "arrogant" hawks and
"humble" sparrows. The primary hurdle in this mission is the acquisition
of some mode of communication with each species. The language of
the hawks, as one might suspect, proves to be audial, thus in its own
way verbal or like verbal language. Ciccilo meditates and listens for an
entire year ("scientifically," as he says, evoking visions of Pasolini the
literary semiotician), finally learning to communicate by whistling.
However, in turning from the hawks to the sparrows he experiences a
failure of his "scientific" method: the sparrows do not seem to communicate audially; their method is wholly different from that of their
cousins and thus inaccessible by the rational methods (or semiology, by
way of the metaphor) employed in regard to the hawks. Ciccilo finally
gives up the old method and, thus open to suggestion, makes an
inspired connection ("faith," as he calls it) from watching Nino play
hopscotch. He discovers the language of the sparrows to be visual and
gestural, something like mime (and, of course, cinema).

The trials and discoveries of Ciccilo clearly manifest a shift in linguistic consciousness from verbal to visual orientation and suggest, moreover, in the transition from science to faith by Ciccilo, a shift in consciousness from the rational to the imaginative (imagination suggesting both vision and mystery).[5] As an allegory, Ciccilo's story embodies Pasolini's own sense of moving from literature to cinema and the need to free cinematic discourse from inapplicable verbal/rational assumptions (that images "mean" as do words, and by extension, that ideology clarifies all of experience). "Marxism answers only so far," he notes in his discussion with John Bragin, "then mystery takes over."[6] Likewise, words explain so much but we are left with the irrational aspect of life— cinematically, with the irrationality of the image.[7]

If the process of the Ciccilo/Nino story portrays a shift from verbal to visual orientation and a correlative development in consciousness, we might expect this shift to provide a model for the larger narrative process of the film, and, indeed, I think it does. The film contains approximately twelve episodes by which its own shift in linguistic emphasis divides it neatly in halves of six and six, the first portion concluding in that episode in which Toto, as a tyrannical landlord, threatens his tenants with foreclosure. The following scene, with its bizarre group of Felliniesque people (Pasolini claims a deliberate parody of Fellini here)[8] and their car with the words "flying spectacle" written on it, following as it does the rather realistic setting of the landlord scene, denotes an obvious shift in style by which the visual nature of the frame composition gains emphasis. This shift suggests this transition to be a pivotal point in the film, a movement perhaps from verbal to visual dominance, and indeed the first six episodes do share a concern with verbal communication, while the last six are structured upon increasing infusions of visual experience. The first half of the film, for example, is marked by the dominance of the crow, a dominance expressed in his verbal admonitions and the story he tells which, though visualized for us, keeps the images in a role as functions of the words. With his word orientation, of course, comes a corresponding interest in ideology, by its emphasis on abstract order, a form of rationalism. What the crow wishes to effect is a control of change by conforming motion to the laws of ideology. To some degree, his method is mirrored by the tavern proprietor who offers to "teach" Nino to dance. Rather than urging him to respond naturally to the rhythm or to assimilate the movements visually, he tells him to regulate his movements to a metronomic system: "Count the steps or you won't learn." This verbal/rationalist approach to change generally characterizes action in the first portion of the film.

The episode following the tavern scene develops the issue of word dominance in a slightly different way, suggesting that such dominance leads to a split between discourse and perception (i.e., words either lie or prove inadequate in the face of mortality). Toto and Nino come upon a group of people standing quietly around a house. Toto seeks a verbal explanation for the circumstances, but is answered with silence and ambiguous nods. He is denied verbal communication and is left with the use of his eyes to figure things out (Nino, interestingly, stands directly behind Toto in such a way as to isolate his eyes). Eventually, Toto witnesses a dead woman brought from the house with still no explanation provided; one feels as Toto does, that words in the face of death become superfluous, as they must in the face of all mysteries. What is conveyed visually is finally what is significant and what one is left with.

If Toto's experience confronts us with the limitation of verbal language, Nino's confronts us with the possibilities of its misuse—or at least the manner by which it lends itself to distortion. Nino departs the death scene to visit a girl friend, whom he finds donning a pair of angel wings in a junk yard. He engages her in a conversation which becomes a conflict between what has been seen and what Nino verbally claims has occurred:

> GIRL: They saw you with a girlfriend of mine.
> NINO: Yeah, I saw her and we chatted.
> GIRL: Yes, in the fields she told me.
> NINO: What fields? We went that way because her father slaps her . . . get it?

Nino's rationalizations are met with silence; his girl friend leaves. Her girl friend likewise rejects him, and Nino returns to Toto by running along the ruins of an old aqueduct, an image which corresponds to his psychology, for he is *intellectually* moving along the ruins of an outmoded manner of experiencing.

One is tempted to argue that all Toto and Nino need are better verbal explanations, but these are exactly what the crow provides. Obviously, they do not effect change in Toto and Nino. What happens instead is that the conflict between the abstract pole of language and the physical pole of reality becomes aggravated into violent explosions.

In the episode following the story of Nino and Ciccilo, language is displayed to be a tool of abstract demarcation which causes direct conflict with natural instincts. Toto is moved by the urge to defecate; spying an apparent latrine in a nearby field, he runs to it and relieves himself.

His movements are intercut with a shot of the crow resting on a sign which boldly proclaims the land to be private property. Now clearly on one level what occurs here is a political issue involving the unnatural- ness of private property (man is partially communal, etc.), but at the same time the use of the sign has a McLuhanesque dimension in which the medium is the message. It is the visual progeny of six or seven preceding signs (e.g., "the street of Vito torn sheets"), all used for demarcation of some sort and all appearing in the first half of the film. They become, by their verbal nature, part of the linguistic issue dra- matized in the movie and the results of their usage must be seen as attributes of their nature and part of the process of the film. In essence, the words impose an abstract delineation upon the terrain which is not visible to the eye nor recognizable by the call of nature; given Pasolini's linguistic professions, one is led to see that the problem is not merely with what the words say (the sign could read "public property"), but with their inherent nature: they may provide a tool of reason but also lend themselves to the urge for control and domination. In short, the situation engenders the recognition that both private property and the verbal language necessary to define it are abstractions which, by their use as tools of control, have come into direct conflict with human real- ities. The solution is not to redefine verbally but to reperceive holisti- cally, a state which must be self-generated and not conditioned, which may explain why Toto and Nino never perceivably change from the influence of the crow.

Having confronted the nature of private property from the angle of the disenfranchised, Toto visits his own property in the role of landlord and threatens his tenants with expulsion, having apparently learned nothing. His domination again becomes associated with words by his reliance on the institution of the law, an institution wholly embodied in words, to sustain his claims. But verbal dominance has another inter- esting twist in this scene. The starving children of the woman are kept from feeling the extent of their hunger through the repeated verbal assurance by the woman that it is not yet daylight and, hence, not yet time to eat. Language conditions reality without generating a real solution to the problem. Toto, likewise, ignores the glaring poverty and suffering, absorbed only in the law and personal interest.

In some manner, then, each of these episodes in the first portion of the film generates, either latently or ostensibly, a sense of conflict between verbal and visual language, a conflict in which vision, for the most part, operates only as a function of language. Hence, structurally (in terms of linguistics), the film's first half is concerned with the problem of unity, involving the relationship of the abstract to the concrete, and seems imbued with an existential sense that existence precedes meaning, that words cannot, despite the attempts of the characters, create reality. Experience created by abstractions (language, private property, or "ego") breeds strife; clearly, some ingredient is needed to rejoin the disparate elements—mind/body, idea/concretion. That ingredient takes the form structurally of an unexplained injection of visual imagination into the film which moves the narrative, as in Ciccilo's story, from a predominantly verbal to a predominantly visual process.

Although Toto and Nino have visibly worked nothing out for themselves—nor made any connections—they move into a world in which the word-image relationship is reversed from its previous conditions. Rather than operating as a tool to create reality, language becomes a function of vision and imagination. Hence, upon leaving the house, Toto and Nino encounter a bizarre group of people standing around a painted Cadillac, and we find that the stylistic quality of the film has suddenly shifted from near neo-realist to fantastic. The figures are more creatures of imagination than those of the rather rational tradition of "realism" or the conventional "verbal" sensibility (articulating social injustice) which tends to go with neo-realism. The deliberate Felliniesque style is far indeed from neo-realism. The change in the relationship between word and image consciousness in the film is typified by the manner in which the "spectacular" quality of this new populace is only reinforced for us verbally (the words "flying spectacle" scrawled on the side of the Cadillac) not defined. These words do not create the essence or reality of the scene—that quality inheres in the total stylistic shift—but guide our attention directly into the flow of images.

The emphasis on visuality is maintained in the following episodes with fewer verbal clues to direct our attention. The scene at the engineer's house, which repeats the problems of private ownership, exists in a context quite unlike that of the earlier scenes. The house and party guests are clearly visually fantastical, from the modern Roman with leaves around his head to the band leader conducting a nonexistent orchestra. In this case, the absurdity of the characters is generated from the conflict of their mentality—old world verbal—with their changing environment. (One of the party guests, for example, is a law-obsessed engineer who is lost in pseudo-intellectual chatter about the professorial sources of James Bond novels.) These bearers of the old linguistic mode are anachronistic (note the eighteenth-century paintings) and, in the crow's phrase, "unchanged."

In the following episode Nino and Toto witness a wholly visual event, the funeral of Marxist leader Togliatti, a man for whom Pasolini professed no admiration and whose death he was accordingly prone to see as positive and symbolic.[9] Appropriately, we see actual footage of the funeral intercut into the narrative which, by juxtaposition, garners unto itself an even greater aura of the neo-realist sensibility. It engenders precisely the passing of that order, yet its intrusion into the narrative, by virtue of the absence of verbal explanation, sustains the eruptive visual spirit of the second half of the movie. The passing of the dogmatic political mentality and the neo-realist consciousness is verbally reinforced, after the fact, by the crow's comments on the passing of both Brecht, the father of ideological theater, and Rossellini, the father of neo-realism. We are led to draw the conclusion that Pasolini associates the passing of these spirits with the passing of a political cinema whose easy readability does not challenge the viewer to reflect. A new story, a new form of cinema, seems at hand, each liberated from ideological/rational control, although assimilating their values into its own spirit. Pasolini writes: "Film at first appeared to me to be a new [literary] technique; working with film, on the other hand, I realized film is absolutely a new language; "*Uccelacci Uccellini* [*The Hawks and the Sparrows*] makes explicit the relationship between reason and mystery. Reason answers up to a certain point, but after a certain point it cannot respond, any mystery enters. . . . The Crow responds to many small questions regarding our human horizon: that is, ten years, twenty years, a century or two. To this a Marxist ideologue can respond, but after a certain limit we cannot succeed in answering."[10] All of this suggests not an impending gloom from the death of reason, but an unfolding of new possibilities in cinematic form generated from the visual nature of the medium itself, possibilities already operant in *The Hawks and the Sparrows*, by which the old conventions of linear plot and prominence of character are superseded by the vision of man "as image," as a creature pregnant with explosive possibilities and impenetrable mystery.

What becomes important, then, in regard to change is not what one *says* but what he *does*. Considered in this light, the end of the film makes some sense, for it concludes in two actions of integration (or actualizations of possibility) which are merely absurd if considered from the standpoint of rational assumptions. In essence, Toto and Nino couple with and assimilate embodiments of "mystery" and "reason." The first act occurs through the sexual intercourse of the two with Luna, the woman they encounter sitting on the roadside. Her name, of course, associates her with the moon (and hence the world of night mystery), whose presence has loomed over the narrative from the credit sequence (for which it provides the background), to the initial conversation of Nino and Toto about the moon's control of tides, to the random intercuttings of its image throughout the film. As in the narrative itself, value is relocated from an abstract realm (the distant lunar orbit and invisible pull) to an embodiment in living human form, or from static sign to living image. By coupling with Luna, Nino and Toto finally (and literally) embrace the darkness and mystery they have previously ignored. By then eating the crow (the very symbol of reason), they complete their growth, literally "assimilating" (in Pasolini's own phrase) the crow's rational powers and historical consciousness.

This sense of "coming together," so prominent in the film's finale, may be extended to the characters Nino and Toto. Although father and son, much of their behavior in the film runs at cross-purposes, tending to dissociate rather than unify them. Moreover, each is endowed with radically different impulses. For example, the relationship of the two in the first half of the film is aggravated by opposite qualities (control versus impulse, intellectual versus biological instinct, experience versus innocence). While Toto sits at the bar sipping a Cinzano, Nino runs outside to join the dancers; while Toto stands at the house of death, Nino runs off to visit his girl friend; while (as Ciccilo and Nino) Toto's mind is set on accomplishing the mission, Nino's is on cottage cheese and playing hopscotch. In most of the early scenes their activities tend to split rather than unite them.

This radical differentiation is carried over into the frame composition, for in the opening shots of the two they tend to be shown in separate frames, Toto appearing on the extreme right of his and Nino on the extreme left of his, creating a distinct imbalance. In accordance with his simplicity, Nino is shot in front of almost nonexistent backgrounds (blank sky with an indistinct horizon). In contrast, the backgrounds for Toto, although he is walking close to Nino, are highly complex configurations, primarily of buildings under construction (See illustration).

As an experienced and sarcastic man of the world, Toto is a man of backgrounds, a man more emotionally complex than his son. Nevertheless, he could do with a little of Nino's innocence and spontaneous ability to enjoy life. This, in fact, he seems to acquire by the end of the film in his coupling with Luna.

To a certain degree, the two embody the powers of vision and reason differentiated in the narrative. Toto, by virtue of his invocation of laws and sense of controlled purpose, is the rationalist of the two; Nino, by the greater emphasis on his eyes and his delight in seeing (he is the one who first sees the vision of the funeral), bears the "potentials" of vision. He is often situated on the screen in such a manner that his eyes become his most prominent feature (standing behind Toto at the death house or behind a metal shield at the junk yard). The two begin to integrate their powers gradually in the course of the movie, beginning with the confrontation with the farmers over the use of their private commode. Nino sneaks behind them, to act as a literal tripping block, while Toto fulminates over the principle of private property. Toto is thus enabled to trip the farmers over Nino's body and escape.

Progressively, the experiences of Nino and Toto become shared rather than divided. Each helps push the stalled Cadillac, each is victimized by the engineer's dogs, each experiences the vision of the funeral, each couples with Luna the fertility maid, and each devours the crow; in essence, each begins to acquire qualities he has previously lacked.

In addition to the linguistic and metaphysical levels of the film, we can examine Toto and Nino's integration on the political, or social, level. As the repeated allusions to private property suggest, this "political" union embraces the opposed social identities of the public and the private man. In the first portion of the film, Toto and Nino tend to be detached from their social milieus; Toto is an outsider at the death scene, Nino is a misfit among the rock 'n' roll dancers whom he joins momentarily. Each has an occasional impulse to join a social group (particularly Nino), but each tends to remain aloof. Toto more obviously stands for the claims of the individual private man, ignoring the dancers, the money mongers who commercialize him in his incarnation as a monk, and, when necessary, his own starving tenants. The claims of the private man, made regardless of the "community of man," however, prove inadequate. Ironically, even as a monk, Toto-Ciccilo never unifies the two classes of birds, and, in his "Toto" existence, his blind disregard for certain public, communal claims is reduced to absurdity (as in the private property episode) or revealed as strikingly cruel.

The movement of the narrative from verbal to visual dominance brings with it as well a fusion of the private and public man. Thus in the first episode of the second portion of the film, Toto and Nino respond to a request for help from a microcosmic social group (i.e., they push the Cadillac). That the car has stopped, of course, implies not the arrest of the world but, at least, the limitations of the totally private life, the

Cadillac being the embodiment of the ideal of consumer luxury cherished by the man of private wealth. When the car stops, Toto and Nino expend their energy in a futile effort to start it, revealing the degree of their importance. They are, nevertheless, responding to a plea from other humans, expressing, for the first time, a degree of social responsibility.

Another cut at private property occurs in the allusion to Anibale's common cure, which he will not reveal without a substantial fee. (On the other hand, his private capitalism is partially provoked by Toto's unconscious slur of Anibale's African origin: "My corns hurt like people who walk on fire to burn the spirits of the dead . . . in your country".) As usual, Toto, the consumer/capitalist, reaps what he sows, buying a corn cure which turns out to be a contraceptive. The unit of society pictured here is obviously ideologically uninformed as regards virtuousness in marketing, but it is held together by a reverence for life (even unwanted life) and each other, which warrants the positive conclusion of the episode, a birth and the magical ignition of the stalled automobile.

The people in this episode form a model of society in which each of the members is uniquely individual yet crippled in some way. Within the group the expressions of private growth and public responsibility exist symbiotically. One misses in this model, however, any consciousness of economic necessity (but in that respect no one else in the movie, except the woman making bird's nest soup, has it either). The bizarre group, at any rate, strikes a balance between private necessity and social pressure, the latter of which Toto has forcibly impressed upon him in the adventure at the engineer's house. Most simply, his previous role as landlord is reversed and he finds himself at the mercy of an unconscionable baron of private enterprise—the engineer who chastises him with the phrase which he, Toto, applied to the starving woman, "Business is business."

That Toto has actually learned anything from all of this is certainly dubious but not necessarily the issue. There is no conclusive evidence that Toto assimilates any of his experiences in the film at all. He goes on as before despite the profound changes in the contours of his world, i.e., entire cities razed and raised, private property yielding to social imperatives. (In this regard it is appropriate that Pasolini tends to repeat the medium long shot of the group walking on the road through much of the film. The repetition of the same footage, with new dialogue, defeats any sense of intellectual progress Toto may be making.) The humanistic value of Toto obviously does not lie entirely in the realm of character (i.e., consciousness) but in his activity as an image in a different, more visual, kind of cinema; and the manner of that achievement should be seen, at least, as an attempt on Pasolini's part to create a new kind of story, political, but not like a Brechtian epic, a story more directly and intimately connected with the nature of the medium. As he continues with this new film story Pasolini deals with the Oedipus myth, concerned less with its function as a Freudian fable (its exposition of "character") than with its poetical and epical rendition of a crisis in the evolution of human consciousness.

Lastly, all discussion of the intellectual concerns of *The Hawks and the Sparrows* somehow misses the experiential life of the film which inheres in its sense of humor, at times like that of Buster Keaton, at other times like that of Fellini, but still uniquely Pasolini's. One cannot do justice, for example, to the surprising effect of having the credits sung in the manner of a motet nor of watching Toto speak to the sparrows through hopscotchlike jumps. One only wishes that such humor had surfaced more often.

Edipo Re: *Two classic catastrophes: (top) Franco Citti as Oedipus fighting his father's soldiers; (bottom) Oedipus blinded*
The Museum of Modern Art/Film Stills Archive

6

Oedipus Rex: Consciousness and History

PASOLINI REMARKED THAT "there are moments in history when one cannot be innocent, one must be aware; not to be aware is to be guilty,"[1] when he was making a segment for the compilation film *Amore e Rabbia* (1967). This statement applies to the central characters of all of his films of this period, from Toto in *The Hawks and the Sparrows* to Oedipus and Medea. Despite this fact, *Oedipus Rex* marks a radical departure in Pasolini's work in a number of ways. It is his first feature film shot in color (he had been experimenting with it as early as *La Ricotta*). More importantly, the film is the first in a series dealing not only with issues involving the individual's awareness of historical processes but with the evolution of consciousness itself. *Oedipus Rex, Medea,* and *Teorema,* when placed in this sequence (*Teorema* was actually filmed shortly before *Medea*), form a narrative trilogy tracing the evolution of human consciousness through its mythical, rational, and finally "post-rational" states.

Oedipus Rex, as the first in this trilogy of films, deals with the problems of a myth-oriented consciousness—one defined by the film as having endowed the world with an anthropomorphic spirituality to which it has surrendered its personal identity. Pasolini's Oedipus, unlike Sophocles' hero (who is rather intellectual), brings about his destruction less through uncontrollable fate or subconscious urges than through a willful failure to look into things, to assume, in some degree, a rational intelligence. In terms of evolution, his crisis is that of primitive man confronting the emergence of rational thought, and his actions bespeak a terror of not only the responsibility this emergence entails but his own individuality as well. Much of this was suggested by Pasolini himself in an interview with Oswald Stack:

People in Italy criticized me for not making Oedipus an intellectual, because everyone in Italy imagines Oedipus as an intellectual, but I think that is a mis-

take because an intellectual's vocation is to seek things out; as soon as an intellectual sees something that doesn't work, by vocation he begins to look into it.
Whereas Oedipus is the opposite: he is the person who does not want to look
into things, like all innocent people, those who live their lives as the prey of
life and of their own emotions.[2]

Pasolini's *Oedipus,* then, despite the Freudian overtones of its opening
scene (with the father gripping the feet of his son out of jealousy), is
really more concerned with the nature of innocence, particularly *willed*
innocence by which one tries to protect himself from impinging conditions and is thus destroyed. Cinematically, this issue is translated into a
tension between "interior" and "exterior": the failure of innocence
being a willful surrender to exterior structure for the determination of
his fate, a failure to center his life inside himself. (One thinks immediately of Accatone or Mamma Roma.) A definite movement toward
the interior is established in the opening shots; we begin outside the
city, move across a field to a house, and focus upon a window toward
which the camera begins to track slowly. Yet we never get wholly
inside (nor does Oedipus into himself); the movement is truncated and
we witness, from the outside, the birth of a child we assume to be
Oedipus.

What follows this opening track are a series of episodes invented by
Pasolini. The father's antagonism toward the child is documented, as is
the child's impulse to avoid seeing things; he covers his eyes repeatedly,
a physical tic that will come to characterize Oedipus morally in the film.
But the most significant of the invented scenes is the discus-throwing
contest, for it dramatizes both Oedipus's orientation toward external
approval and his innocence (an innocence which, in fact, substitutes
unintelligent physical response for reflection). Oedipus, in late adoles-
cence, is shown competing with some companions—apparently for
some form of public recognition—while festively clad spectators watch.
Oedipus's discus toss and that of a competitor fall close together. He
races to the site ahead of his companions and nudges his own discus
ahead of the other with his foot (the second suggestive use of that limb
as part of a play upon his name, which means "Swollen Foot").
Accused of cheating, Oedipus bludgeons his opponents into submission
with his fists, establishing his characteristic manner of dealing with
moral issues. Yet despite the substitution of violence for thought, his
egoism has a certain innocent quality to it, for it is not the malicious
will to hurt someone, but more the childish penchant for having his
sense of identity and worth reinforced by public approval. Appropri-

ately, when a crown of wilted flowers is bestowed upon his head, he beams with the pride of unreflecting innocence. He appears to us, here, essentially mindless, physical, and prone to thoughtless acceptance of external conditioning.

In a more subtle way, his reliance upon external authority is made a central part of his motive for visiting the Delphic Oracle through whom he first hears of his fate. Oedipus has a nightmare terrifying enough to compel him to seek an explanation to placate his fear of the dark: "I woke up sobbing and trembling with a fear of the dark I haven't had since I was a child. . . . I stayed awake till dawn, with shivers up because of the fear that the dark and the silence aroused in me. . . . I don't want that dream to come back and torment me. I want to know what it means."

One is tempted to argue here, that Oedipus's words clearly demonstrate a will toward intellectual clarification, but the crux of the issue is that it is not Oedipus who is actually looking into things (for this is what Pasolini means by the term "intellectual," one who assumes the responsibility to understand and clarify). Oedipus characteristically seeks the explanation from someone else—an external authority—and in this capacity he dramatizes the nature and weakness of "mythical consciousness," its manner of conceiving the individual as a total pawn of forces beyond him. It is precisely the achievement of the intellectual to take on the power of the gods, to assume responsibility for himself. Such assumption is an act of self-"internalizing," of individuating oneself within an environment without sundering his consciousness from it. Intellection is thus presented as a force impelling individuation; and by its association with experience and cognizance, Pasolini suggests that innocence (the state Oedipus wishes to retain) is a fear of self, a refusal not only to see *for* oneself but to try to see *into* oneself; his inner life remains a feared experience.

When he does receive an "explanation" from the Oracle, Oedipus accepts it without any reflection and "selects" his itinerary by not selecting at all. When he aimlessly comes upon a crossroads, he chooses a direction by closing his eyes and spinning in a circle, a complete abdication of responsibility. He will not return to Polybus, for he neither knows nor trusts himself. One thinks here, also, of another small scene inserted by Pasolini in this part of the film. Oedipus, wandering about, encounters an old man dancing in a circle (the film's central motion) surrounded by naked boys. The old man beckons Oedipus to pass through a corridor in the ruins beside them and Oedipus complies somnambulistically, a willing pawn of another's will. In a scene charged with mystery, yet entirely consistent with the tenor of the film, Oedipus discovers a barely clad girl at the end of the corridor who comports herself with the air of one expectantly awaiting an inevitable visitor. In fact, the strong suggestion here, given the girl's location, her nakedness, and the old man's pandering, is that she is a prostitute and the old man a sort of pimp. Taken as a comment upon Oedipus's destiny, the scene implies that his failure to act more self-reliantly—his retainment of protective innocence—is merely prostitution.

If his choice of roads seems accidental and mindless, so does his murder of his father. The actual crime is only alluded to in Sophocles and in other versions of the myth, but Pasolini provides a lengthy, detailed treatment of the event. As in the Sophocles story, the two meet on a narrow road and have an argument over the right of way, Laius being by far the most adamant and arrogant character in the film. Oedipus, on the other hand, has no reason for not yielding the way and seems out of control in his obstinacy, for when challenged by Laius's guards, he becomes frightened and flees for his life. He is pursued by the swifter of Laius's soldiers, whom he finally kills in impetuous fear when he can run no further. At the approach of a second soldier, Oedipus again retreats in fear, then slowly, suffering a change of mind, kills that soldier as well. Each success fuels his blood-lust until he has massacred the king and his retinue. Appropriately, he slaughters the king with no verbal confrontation at all. That is, as the scene is presented—an absurd clash of unrelenting egos—even the viewer feels the need of some explanation for the king's behavior and is left with a stark sense that the incident which ignited the fury, being incredibly minor, could easily have been avoided with a little negotiation by either party. Neither figure ever explains himself nor seeks an explanation from the others. Are we to believe they subconsciously recognize and hate each other? Perhaps such was the Freudian intent; but on screen the fight is largely one between mindless bodies, each attempting to exert physical ascendancy over the other. Each acts as if controlled by a destiny beyond his will which he is incapable of comprehending. Oedipus, particularly, seems no longer capable of self-generated activity (as in his cheating at the discus-throwing contest), for he now lacks the capacity to influence his own life.

The intellectual failure of Pasolini's Oedipus (with the attendant issue of internalized responsibility) is nowhere clearer than in his confrontation with the Sphinx. In the Sophocles version, of course, Oedipus solves a riddle posed by the Sphinx, an act which to some degree establishes his credentials as an intellectual or a thinker. (Joseph Campbell's influ-

ential view of the Sophocles play in *The Hero with a Thousand Faces*
envisions Oedipus as an intellectual force striving to evade its naturalis-
tic roots.) Pasolini's Oedipus solves no riddles nor does he have any posed
(in fact, one of the major problems with the film is that the Sphinx is
given no function or explanation). He deals with the Sphinx as he deals
with everything else, by using physical power. There is in his victory,
moreover, the strong suggestion of a desire to repress understanding and
intellect. Although the role of the Sphinx in the Theban world is vague,
his very knowledge of Oedipus and his querying endow him with almost
symbolic status as a force of rational power:

> SPHINX: There is an enigma in your life. What is it?
> OEDIPUS: I don't know. I don't want to know.

The intellectual nature of the Sphinx is rather more explicit in the
screenplay, but regardless, what he offers Oedipus is the invitation to
pursue his nature, and Oedipus's refusal to do so becomes a denial of
emergent intelligence and rationality—an arid refusal to grow. Oedipus
literally opts for innocence and self-ignorance, contrary to Pasolini's
insistence that "there are moments in history when one cannot be
innocent."

The exchange between Oedipus and the Sphinx has an interesting
twist to it: the confusion of external form with internal reality. While
Oedipus screams, "I don't want to see you!" the Sphinx retorts, "The
abyss you are pushing me into is within yourself." This reply has a
number of intriguing implications. It strongly reinforces the symbolic
role of the Sphinx as an agent of precipitant rationality and affirms that
force is being repressed by a primitive mind afraid to understand itself.
In addition, the mere fact of its externalized appearance yet internal
reality defines the conditions of spiritual vision in the mythical world,
i.e., that for Pasolini these figures are externalized representations of
man's own powers. Accordingly, in order for man to assume them con-
sciously he must murder them as externalized symbols, a necessary
slaughter encumbent upon the ascension to intellectual, rational control
of his destiny, but it is a slaughter with traumatic effects. Yet as the
sphinx suggests Oedipus, even as he attempts to reject this invitation to
self-reliant thought, inadvertently assumes the power into himself. And
perhaps because it is repressed in the assimilation, a violent breakdown
ensues. Hence from the wedding bed of Oedipus and Jocasta (itself
following closely on the heels of the killing of the Sphinx) Pasolini cuts

to the dead and blistered bodies of the Thebans lying about the town. The plague thus has a historical, "causal" sense to it, a rather symbolic sense, in that Oedipus's murder of the Sphinx (regardless of how one interprets it) engenders the very destruction of that which Oedipus sought to preserve: physicality. Placed upon a scale of evolutionary history, Pasolini's version of the Oedipus myth becomes the story of man's taking into himself the symbols which he formerly projected onto his world, and, in a slightly different manner, his futile attempt to reject his role in their creation and in so doing reject the rational responsibility for his individual destiny. It is this sense in which Oedipus fails to be in touch with the historical moment. The body dies as the center of human identity with the relentless emergence of intellectual, rational thought. Blindness, a separation of awareness from the physical world, is made part and parcel of intellectual blossoming in Pasolini's version.

Although the awareness of his identity is forced upon him, and although he blinds himself from the guilt he feels in having coupled with his mother, Oedipus never really makes the transition to rational consciousness. His understanding is too late and is imposed from the outside. He becomes, at film's end, an absurd figure out of touch with the world of factories and apartment buildings through which he wanders blindly with his flute.

The fact that Oedipus ends his journey in the contemporary, rather than the ancient, world reminds us of the "sandwich" construction of the film. The larger portion of Oedipus's experience is filmed in a locale suggestive of the ancient world of the Sophocles story. However, the beginning and end of the film occur in modern Italy, the opening in the military state of prewar Fascist Italy, the end in the Italy of 1967. This sandwiching lends itself to a number of interpretations. On the one hand, it invites a sort of Freudian view of the film, with Oedipus's life becoming the metahistorical archetype submerged in the consciousness of modern man. And insofar as the Freudian dimensions of the story are unavoidable, this view makes sense. Yet the film's other issues, coupled with Pasolini's minimizing of the Freudian elements in the film, suggest that the structure may serve other functions: "I am no longer seriously involved in the academic bog which turns Oedipus into a whipping post for Freudian or Marxist theories."[3]

One function the structure serves is the casting of a time frame around the major portion of the story. With reference to the modern world in which he lives, Oedipus's life is out of synchronization with his time. But the frame also suggests the imposition of externally imposed controls on his life, not unlike the conditions under which he has labored in life. The framing pattern is sustained in the imagery of the film. Our first glimpse of Oedipus, for example, is as a newborn child within the frame of the bedroom window. This is extended to the frame of the crib and the grid of the field where he throws the discus. On the morning after his nightmare, he is seated in the palace; the camera moves back slowly to reveal his figure neatly framed by door lintels. What movement he does make in open space is nullified by the inevitable return to a controlling square or situation. His initial wanderings lead to a confined square with a strange girl and his argument with Laius is held over the right of way to a narrow road in the middle of nowhere. There is infinite room for either to pass the other without even being in sight; yet each man's perception is defined by the imposed limitations of the roadway.

Oedipus becomes king only to be forced to sit in the frame of a baroque window of the palace, and the shots of him at the industrial site at film's end, taken in geometrical perspective like those of *Accatone*, suggest his confinement. His final locale is the field of his childhood, which is a square demarcated by rows of trees. Oedipus thus not only ends where he begins, but ends still as a pawn of destiny, an innocent whose refusal to aspire to self-knowledge has cast a net around his actions from which he cannot escape.

The geometrically inclined may see the film as a merger of two forms, the square and the circle, for while Oedipus operates within the enclosure of a frame, he also comes "full circle" at film's end, returning to his origin in an act which amplifies all of his circular behavior throughout the film (spinning at the crossroads, circling from Thebes to Corinth and back to Thebes). In either context, self-enclosure (without prompt self-knowledge) serves to describe the condition of his existence. He remains lost in a state of consciousness both pre-Christian and outside historical process. One thinks of the final lines of Pasolini's poem "L'appennino:"

> he shuts his eyelids
> in ignorance, and is lost in a people
> whose clamor is nothing but silence.

7

Medea:
Myth and Reason

IF *OEDIPUS REX* PORTRAYS the enclosure of primitive mentality in
a limbo outside historical change, *Medea* is concerned with the collision
of mythological with modern, or specifically rational, consciousness. It
deals less with the personality differences of two individuals than with
a transition in human consciousness on a large scale. Regarding this,
Pasolini notes, "Jason and Medea . . . are one and the same character."[1]
However, on the personal level, Jason unifies the narrative by his growth
through both stages of consciousness. As the story develops around Jason,
it generates, as well, a changing image of the role and function of narrative in human history: from that of reconciling man with nature to
that of impelling the growth of the individual from collective to personal
consciousness.

Stages in the Legend

The opening episode, in both style and theme, creates a model for the
transition in consciousness depicted by the film. The sequence begins
with the infant Jason, sitting in a patch of light inside the doorway of a
small hut. The camera also is enclosed in the hovel, focused upon a centaur who lectures Jason about his origin and destiny. As the scene pro-
gresses, both camera and characters move gradually toward the light of
the exterior world. At the episode's conclusion, we, Jason, and the centaur stand on the shores of an ocean, gazing raptly into infinite space, on
the threshold of an unexplored world. There is, thus, for both audience
and characters a gradual expansion of vision from the hermetic world
of the hut to the world at large.

To some degree, this shift is inherent in the change of consciousness
marked by the centaur's talk. Initially, he describes for us a reverential
but mythological sense of nature not unlike that which Pasolini speaks
of in regard to *The Gospel According to Matthew.* When the centaur

95

looks upon the world, he sees not a machine governed by physical laws, but a vital, living organism in which every visible form is sustained by a spiritual presence: "All is sacred, All is sacred. There is nothing natural in nature.... Does a piece of that sky seem unnatural and possessed by a God.... Wherever your eye roams a God is hidden."

The anthropomorphic nature of that presence, however, is a measure of the limitations of the vision, of myth consciousness. To a certain degree sacredness is in the eye of the beholder, for as the episode proceeds and Jason grows to manhood, we discover that the centaur's vision of nature is significantly fictive, not the perception of an absolute external condition but a conscious, imaginative construction in which religious faith operates as a tool to induce spiritual vision. Hence, the episode concludes with the centaur's explanation that under the scrutiny of the "new" reason the old analogies between man and nature (seeds and human resurrection) "no longer have any meaning." "In fact," he concludes, "there is no God." The crisis confronting Jason, which he does not understand, is precisely how to reconcile the two forms of perception exposed by the centaur (the mystical and the rational), or, in terms more relevant to a modern audience, how are we to operate in the world with the freedom gained from the birth of reason without sacrificing the spiritual vision of reality inspired by the old religion?

Jason does not fare well at making the reconciliation; his reason becomes a tool for making business deals. But Pasolini does not present a one-sided picture of the conflict between the two modes of consciousness. The initial episode moves toward enlarged rational vision, but before we can witness the further development of the new perception, the film cuts directly to a more "primitive" society in which the contours of a literal, primitive myth-consciousness can be seen.

Mythological man, in true Pasolini fashion, achieves a sense of vivid spiritual immediacy through his anthropomorphic vision, but he does so by enclosing himself hermetically in a world of static symbols. He becomes prey to outside forces of change and to the latent individuative urges suppressed by his religion. Medea's world, for example, is a closed system, centered on and organized around a static symbol, the fleece of a goat. In essence, the spiritual presence in nature is wholly externalized in an iconic object which freezes consciousness and becomes ready prey to forces which might impinge upon and destroy it. Moreover, as the symbol gains power over human consciousness, it engenders an essentially propitiatory need of dealing with the gods of nature, a need that results in human sacrifice. As the centaur notes, "The Gods that love, at the same time hate." Hence, our introduction to the mythological world of Medea comes by way of a sacrificial rite of spring in which the blood of a victim is used as a catalyst to impel the fertility of the land. Likewise, the vineyard trees are clustered with wine jugs symbolically hung to inspire a rich harvest. It is a land in which objects are invested by faith with magical powers.

Despite its sacrificial core, however, the symbolic orientation of Medea's world renders it a land rich in color and beauty. The shapes which define it, such as the shrine of the goat, the contours of the dwellings, and the symbols carried by the participants in the rite are irregular, gothic, and primarily curvilinear, suggestive of the irrational consciousness from which they flow. By contrast (in accordance with the collision at the heart of the film), Jason's explorations are marked by geometrical form and rational linearity. The shot of his arrival at his uncle's island, for example, stresses the perfect alignment of his men along the beach. In our next vision of them, they are perfectly aligned horizontally across the screen. As a bearer of reason, Jason thus introduces perspective and linear formation into the world and with it a degree of control over nature lacking in the myth-oriented cultures.

Moreover, despite the rigid profiles of his group, Jason also introduces something else, a capacity for directional movement lacking in both Medea's world and his own preadolescent island. The sacred vision of the centaur (in line with what we see) is largely based on stillness, "the stillness of a summer sky" or "the clouds reflected in the calm, still water at three in the afternoon." Indeed, the most motion perceivable in the scenes of Jason's youth occurs when he plays with a sand crab. If Medea's world seems, by contrast, effervescent, its vitality is based on motion which is largely ritualized and constrained. This motion is cyclical, like that of the wheel Medea spins, and centered upon essentially static, or repeating, forms. Moreover, as the heavy clothing suggests, it is a world in which the patina of ritual and control suppresses any natural instincts for personal definition. One thinks here not only of the obscured faces of the people (or the painting of the victim), but of the royal family itself, forced to conform to an inherited, definitive role, standing still and unmoving in their abode, framed individually in a series of arched windows. One functions not as a self-sufficient agent in this world, but in terms of an inherited structure which draws definite boundaries around his/her natural mobility. Everyone is, in a sense, the sacrificial victim in the rite of spring, for the prevailing constraint upon motion is indeed a constraint upon individuation and personal identity.

What Jason brings into this world is a vitality of linear motion, a sense of personal power, and a new historical sense which perceives time not in terms of recurring cycles but as a linear process and progression, open-ended and capable of being initiated by an individual. Although his journey begins under the aegis of inherited destiny (to capture a symbol), Jason transforms it into a quest for "experience" valuable in its own right. He ultimately throws the sought-after fleece at his uncle's feet, proclaiming it to be meaningless outside its own country and disavowing any claim to his uncle's empire because "I discovered the world is far wider than your kingdom."

For Jason, motion, rather than symbol, is the dominant force in his life-style,[2] and in the process of being liberated from stillness and static form, he comes to see the world not as a system of absolute roles but as a range upon which he himself is the centering force. Thus, Medea will criticize his camp site: "You are not seeking the center, not marking the center." Liberated from static form and symbol, Jason's men easily carry out their mission, fleeing to their boat while the king's army is immobilized in the ritual of collecting the prince's body. Jason's mobility further liberates him from the quest for inheritance enjoined upon him by the centaur. He moves beyond primitive perception and a sense of identity conditioned by the past (only to arrive in Corinth to join the new establishment rapidly congealing into a bourgeois stasis of its own). Jason's real crime, for Pasolini, is that he stops growing; he severs his ties to the primitive God who once inhabited his consciousness and to the "religious" sentiments—imaginings—which, when released from their anthropomorphic prison, might impel his consciousness to synthesize rational and mystical perception.

Whatever his shortcomings, Jason exudes a sense of vitality to Medea capable of inspiring her to break free of her own hermetic world, at least temporarily. He releases her suppressed impulses for individual destiny. But for Medea, the reconciliation of Jason's rational world with her own proves impossible. The linear forms which endow Jason's life with a degree of liberty become for her a trap and a death sentence. As she wanders along the beach the first night of her departure, the land around her appears as a parched grid, a dry checkerboard of linear form in which the old "God" has been replaced by the form's reason: "Earth, where is your meaning . . . where is your link to the sun?" She perceives that Jason has broken with nature—for him it is no longer an analogue to human life—but cannot herself accept such a split.

The bifurcation in Jason's relationship to nature is a division of consciousness as well, a condition dramatized in the dualistic visitation of the centaur upon his return to Corinth. The centaur appears in two forms, only one of which is that of a centaur, the other being that of a man. It is significant that Jason is informed by this vision that each form has been produced by himself: "It is you who produced it. We are inside you; a sacred one when you were a boy; a desecrated one when you became a man. What was sacred is preserved beside the new desecrated form." In a sense, Jason has arrived at a condition of dualistic perception related to that of Accatone. But where Accatone tended to separate spirit and flesh, Jason divides one historical form of consciousness—irrational, symbolic, and propitiatory—from another—rational, mechanistic, and "human-centered." Both possibilities exist side by side, yet Jason largely denies the urges of the old form, saying, "What use is it to me to know all this?"

Jason has become man in the historical "humanistic" vision, a rational animal placed at the center of his universe[3]—or making himself that center. But in Pasolini's vision this is not enough, for this replacement of symbol with individual soon leads to replacing the individual with reason itself, reducing man to an object in a devitalized expanse. By his very rationality, man removes himself from his spiritually energetic and creative origins in nature. He stands outside nature, fostering a dualistic, subject-object relationship to life which, by its violation of the irrational foundations of life, breeds catastrophe. The solution is not to go back, but to go forward, beyond rationalism, to creative consciousness, a deed not wholly achieved in Pasolini's works until *The Arabian Nights*. Jason's consciousness, blind to a large portion of reality, converts itself into bourgeois materialism, and he ultimately chooses to remarry with the king's daughter, Glauce, in order to improve his station (and that of his children) in bourgeois Corinthian society. This stodgy ideal is to be achieved by leaving Medea behind. Hence, love and passion disappear from the world, having been converted into merchandise.

Narratively, by this point in the film we have passed through two stages of human history, a collision of forms of consciousness, and a bifurcation of perception engendered in the emergence of rational man. In the episodes of Glauce's death, the consequences of rational conscious ness are made manifest: specifically, as "conscience" and moral guilt. Such guilt is based not upon the recognition of a violation of divine law but upon those human rites dependent largely upon the humanistic sense of man as a rational center of the world. Glauce commits suicide because she feels guilty for stealing Medea's husband. In Medea's world, however, this sense of guilt does not exist. Men can be sacrificed and brothers slaughtered without remorse, for such actions are those of the Gods and can be atoned for through the agencies of ritual or the intervention of divine providence. Man is not a center; he must conform to one.

For Glauce, however, no such external form of expiation exists. She dwells solely with her guilt, and her suicide, from a modern perspective, is psychologically and humanistically apt. She leaps from the ramparts of the castle, a small figure against a vast, rather blank background, and dies. From Medea's primitive vision, however, the death is charged with magic and supernatural power. The psychological discomfort of Glauce becomes literal flame for Medea, when in another vision of Glauce's death the garments Medea sends Glauce as a wedding present burst into fire when donned, and Glauce and father perish in the flames of divine retribution.

The two versions of the death, being directly juxtaposed, may confuse viewers, but, in actuality, the double view juxtaposes the two forms of consciousness and carries forward the consequences of their bifurcation. Each vision is true from one point of view because reality in the film is, itself, fictive, dependent upon the manner in which the imagination chooses to create it rather than being a totally absolute "given." They are accordingly different; art is not entirely metahistorical, for the human story changes radically in cultures of different consciousnesses.

Narration

To suggest that the film promotes a fictive or nonabsolute sense of reality is not to condemn it, but rather to locate it more firmly in a contemporary world view in which no absolute reality has been discovered behind the phenomenal world and truth, at least since Nietzsche, has been seen to be a function of our life goals. But these are latent, rather than explicit, conditions in the universe of Medea. What is obvious, however, is the film's recurring concerns with fiction, narrative, and lies.

One of the centaur's first revelations to Jason is the disclosure of his previous misrepresentation of the child's parentage: "You are not my son nor did I find you in the sea." But the lies do not stop here. After the centaur's long prelude in regard to the presence of gods in nature, he closes the first episode with a denial of gods. While he accurately foresees the labors enjoined upon Jason by his uncle, the goat skin itself proves useless and the real value of Jason's adventure proves not to inhere in the centaur's early goals but in the experience of growth itself.

Besides the centaur's deception, there is Medea's duplicity at film's end, the double vision, and the centaur's complicated narrative spun in the opening scene. The film is obsessed with storytelling and thus calls attention to its own narrative structure as being in some way (with a nod to McLuhan) part of the "message" or thematic interest. What becomes important in all of these fictions is not their absolute truth but their operative value, the ability to generate holistic perception or individual growth. Underlying the film is the implied sensibility that the universe is itself neither an absolute pantheon of gods nor a rational system but a creator or storymaker. Truths become useful fictions by which we live, different forms of fiction.

It is the compelling narrative of the centaur that explodes Jason from his hermetic life, causes him to rupture another closed culture, and, in short, sets modern history in motion. It is creative fantasy that fuels evolution and change, rather than, as one might expect in Pasolini, Marxist dialectic. (But, as was noted in the previous chapter, Pasolini had clearly qualified his Marxist affinities by the late 1960s.) Within the context of an essentially fictive universe (and there is no guarantee that Jason's rational perceptions are less fictive than Medea's mythological consciousness), both Jason and Medea become the narrators of their own lives and thus, in an important sense, become what they choose to make themselves. For Medea, unable to accept either Jason's betrayal or exile into a world she cannot comprehend, the choice is regression, and she weaves a narrative of self-destruction—one, however, in which she reclaims her lost sense of kinship with nature. Her betrayal by Jason embodies his severance from his own irrational dimension, a tributary source of his initial adventurousness and "narrative power." As a narrator, he opts for a marriage to a system in which his fictive powers would be shut down, in its own way an act of self-destruction and a refusal to carry forward the narrative impulse as its own end and purpose. He chooses to wed himself to the historical by-product of rational consciousness, the stable, bourgeois, mercantile society.[4] Hence, by the end of the film, the two narrative impulses, mythological and rational (and their counterparts in forms of consciousness), have been irrevocably split and self-defeating. Medea and her children burn while Jason watches helplessly. But, significantly, the rational society of Corinth never wholly denies the power and potential of Medea's form of consciousness; because they no longer understand it, they choose to repress and exile it. In fact, they are afraid of it, as bourgeois society fears any real spiritual perception. Its forms of perception are never wholly discredited within the film itself. It is "profaned" perhaps, but not eradicated.

The film ends with Jason and Medea shouting at each other across the unbridgeable gap of their different worlds as the house and children go up in flames. Medea's final words, "Nothing is possible anymore," testify to the failure of her imagination, her inability to carry forward the narration of her own life. Trapped in the mythological cycle of jealousy and retribution, her life ends in passion and fire, but also in the negation of life. She has failed to grow and thus thwarts growth in others, killing her own children to inflict suffering on Jason. Her failure to grow is consistent with the veneration of stasis which permeates mythological consciousness in the film. And this sense of arrest is implicit in the freeze frame of the sun rising with which the film begins and ends.

In conclusion, the film brings us to the disjunction of two forms of consciousness by way of the severance of Jason and Medea. Jason, though he may not be particularly "savory," still bears the possibility of reconciliation within him in the form of the old and new centaur. His identification with the latter has resulted in a profanation of the former, but if we believe the centaur, the old form remains, though dormant, as a source of holistic vision and creative inspiration.

8

Teorema: Line and Surface

"THE MYSTERY OF THE WORLD is the visible, not the invisible," quips Oscar Wilde. *Teorema* recalls his epigram. The plot meanders with a degree of eccentricity unusual even for Pasolini. A typical audience is usually delighted enough by the film's exoticism to relinquish its concern with how it all adds up—a reaction not unlike that given *Fellini Satyricon* (1967), which *Teorema* actually resembles in significant ways. Each film, for example, features a protagonist who seems hardly to be a character at all; they are, by conventional standards, superficial. Along with this depthlessness of the protagonist, each film is curiously interested in surfaces, in reality itself as a surface: *Fellini Satyricon,* in its concluding frescoes and frescolike mise-en-scène; *Teorema,* in its characters' compulsive interest in surface arts (painting and photography), and in its recurring friezelike frame compositions. Each film, moreover, exposes the collapse of a bourgeois society imaginatively withered by obsessive rationality. Because it deals both with the failure of rational consciousness and with the emergence of a nebulous but more holistic awareness, *Teorema* is thematically the sequel to *Medea* (a film about the ascendancy of bourgeois rationalism) and the terminal chapter in the trilogy of history begun with *Oedipus Rex.*

Technically, *Teorema* takes its title from the theoremlike efficiency with which it demonstrates that the bourgeoisie, no matter how prodigious its efforts, will prove incapable of liberating itself from its own "bourgeoisness."[1] Yet, because of the temptation to deal with *Teorema* strictly as a political allegory (which it partially is), it is well to recall Pasolini's own declaration (made during the writing of *Teorema*) of his emancipation from dogmatic Marxism: "I want to stress the fact that now, at forty-five years of age, I have emerged from the wilderness of Freudian and Marxist dogma."[2] In light of such statements (of which

105

this is only one), it strikes me as absurd that many critics somnambulistically keep affirming that this film is a balance between Pasolini's Freudian and Marxist interests.[3] In fact, it is only tangentially concerned with either. The film's central character (played by the internationally famous actor Terence Stamp) in no way embodies Freudian problems—he is entirely without past or psychological neurosis—nor are the sexual instincts he arouses in the bourgeois family "particularly" of Freudian interest. Neither does he promote any Marxist doctrines, unless ego-less love can now be claimed as the private property of the political left. If anything, the Stamp figure resembles Christ[4] and suggests, in this capacity, that the moral/aesthetic center of the film is once again Pasolini's spiritual engrossment in the nature and permutations of holistic consciousness.

At its spiritual center, the film flourishes with much the same point of view integral to *Accatone, Mamma Roma*, et al.: the individual's need to engender through his own creative powers a holistic vision of life, expanding his capacities for love and self-generation. As always, this individuation is dependent upon the connection between the individual and his world, the process of his being-in-the-world, so to speak. But this relationship is endowed with a peculiarly modern aspect in *Teorema* only marginally present in the earlier films: the growing presence of surfaces in man's world, coupled with the twentieth-century sense that the impermeable, underlying "absolute," once believed to support sensory reality, has dissolved under the eye of science, leaving a universe of plastic surfaces pregnant with creative energy. In a phrase, the universe has melted into light, leaving man without a foundation upon which to establish a stable, fixed identity, but offering him in compensation the invitation to greater deployment of his own fictive powers in the shaping of his destiny.

Surface Consciousness in the Modern World

The surfacity of the modern world has been the subject of a great deal of recent study, some of which may help to throw light on the moral and stylistic peculiarities of *Teorema*. In a recent essay tracing the development of "linear" thought in the West, Richard Palmer has emphasized the connection between the advent of perspectival perception (as evidenced in painting) and the rise of nationalism.[5] Palmer suggests that the geometrical linearity of perspectival thinking made possible a belief in the control of space and, contingent with this, the still prevalent view of man as a reasoner who fulfills himself through establishing a fixed and controlling relationship to his world. In the Age of Reason, this perspectival emphasis led to a disregard of the surface of things, a surgical division of reality between primary qualities—the enduring forms behind the surface of things whose reality is perceivable by reason—and the secondary qualities—the accidents of appearance, mutable and insubstantial, in effect, not real. Palmer adds that this "logocentrism" has passed out of much scientific and philosophical thinking yet persists as a psychic residue in the spiritual attitudes of society. Logocentrism, he suggests, was one form of fictional perception now obsolete in a world whose mystery lies in the nature of its appearance.

These views, in fact, permeate most twentieth century philosophy and science. For example, in his monumental *Being and Nothingness,* Jean-Paul Sartre feels compelled to direct himself to this issue from the very outset of the book:

There is no longer an exterior for the existent if one means by that a superficial covering which hides from sight the true nature of the object. And this true nature in turn, if it is to be the secret reality of the thing, which one can have a presentment of or which one can suppose but never reach because it is the "interior" of the object under consideration—this nature no longer exists. The appearances which manifest the existent are neither interior nor exterior; they are all equal, for they all refer to other appearances, and none of them is privileged.[6]

With the departure of the surface/depth dualism in scientific thought, we have also witnessed the vanishing of perspectival emphasis in the arts, at least as a dominant form. Modern painting, like science, seems devoted to the simultaneity of phenomena rather than to the abstract spatial configurations of them in a field of depth, the mimetic reflection of "reality." Instead, the world of surface reality becomes a presentation of objects and events with self-integrity, yet organically bound with the rest of existence. The relevance of this trend for the narrative arts has been felt by a number of literary figures, Robbe-Grillet and Samuel Beckett, for example. For these writers, the end of our ability to maintain the depth/surface dualism in scientific thinking has been carried over to human thinking, or thinking about man. The indissoluble inner core of human character, presumed, for example, in nineteenth-century literature and common cultural habit, can no longer be said to be really there. Character as the permanent mark of identity, the determining organ of behavior, the "self," may in fact not exist outside of its manifestation as an organic process.[7]

Man as a surface, however, is not necessarily man without consciousness; the loss of character makes possible the liberation of man as creator; and insofar as it carries with it the loss of ego, his presumed rational, irreducible fortress of self, it dissolves the traditional "subject/object" relationship with his world inherent in the logocentric (surface/depth) concept of reality. Man as a surface becomes a process of mutually shared creative responses with his world, individuated yet spiritually and organically related.

However, my purpose here is not polemical but descriptive, since the ideas go far to clarify the moral issues in *Teorema*. Pasolini has drawn for us a portrait of a world in which a new surface consciousness is precipitant even while an old rational order dies; this old order is shown to be explicitly bourgeois, since both rationalism and middle-class goals for Pasolini assume the mental, industrial control of nature by man to be his presiding "good" and both produce conditions of psychic contraction by disregarding the spirituality which infuses consciousness. In imagining man as surface (and thereby abolishing the mental/physical split of rationalism), Pasolini achieves the integral vision he has sought, and achieves it in a medium which, by its nature, authenticates it. For film cannot but incarnate man in light as a vital surface acting from no other depths but his own life force, an apparition at home in a universe of light, consubstantial with it.

The tension between the two visions (rationalism and surfacity) asserts its presence in *Teorema* in a number of ways. Compositionally, Pasolini has shaped the visual style of his story upon the juxtaposition of perspectival vision with radically different surface vision. That is, the film, in its frame composition, proposes two forms of spatial organization, one stressing depth-of-field and the geometrical one-point perspectival relationship of content, as in the opening shots of the factory (See illustration), and a second, in a shot immediately following, in which the depth-of-field effect is flattened into a sheer two-dimensional plane, as when we see the workers pass through the window frames of the factory (See illustration).

Extreme, and therefore obvious, examples of the two distinct compositional possibilities alternate with a stylistic elasticity all through the opening minutes of the film; one mode crystallizes, then dissolves into its opposite. Thus, the factory window shots are followed by a sequence of frames made with a hand-held camera. We seem to be, documentarily,

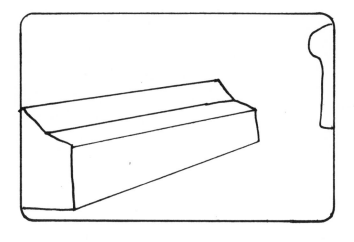

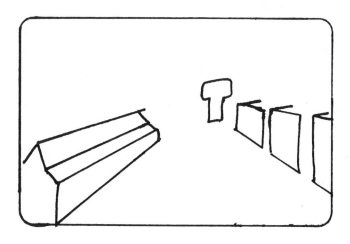

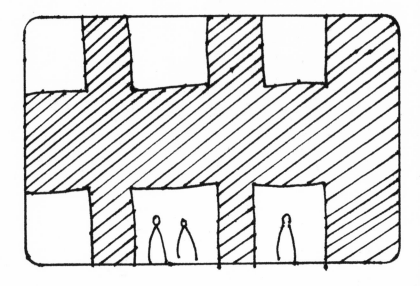

on the location of some disruption at the factory. The organization of space is once again perspectival and depth-oriented. We observe, through serrated rows of human heads, an anonymous figure toward whom all of the attention is directed. As the camera creeps in on this man, the depth-of-field decreases to virtually zero. Then, suddenly, the film cuts to its credit sequence, which is based upon total surface; in fact, the effect is so pronounced as to suggest that this sequence is an allegorical model of cinema itself. Across a flat (slightly undulating) stretch of sand, cloud shadows move. Over both slip the titles. Insofar as we define "movie" as moving shadows on a screen resulting from the transmission of light through a film, then these images comprise a model of that condition, cinema taking itself as its own subject, becoming meta-cinema. As I have tried to suggest, the point in doing this is not to wallow with sheer delight in intellectual gamesmanship, but to present the world suddenly joined with, or in league with, the medium, blurring the distinctions between art and life, message and form.

Styling the Narrative

The extremely tabular quality of the credit sequence yields to perspectival depth as the action returns. We see almost the exact shot of the factories (which launched the film) in radical one-point perspective; yet this time we find ourselves moving within a car toward the vanishing point, where the perspectival lines converge. After a close-up of the car's occupant, we return to the external world to find it perfectly flat again. Suddenly, out of this simultaneity of flatness in which forms coexist with equal power, the camera selects one person for attention, and as it follows this figure, the context changes to a corridor of trees, a walkway which reasserts the spatial organization and differentiation of importance in the figures. This figure is Pietro, the son of the factory owner, Paolo, who was the car's occupant. Pietro's presence gives way abruptly to that of his sister, Odetta. The same shifting between radically identifiable modes of frame composition may again be easily detected. Each family member is introduced in this way and the presentations conclude at the dinner table, where we find them arranged in the familiar symmetry of the one-point perspective: lifeless, impersonal slots in a formal pattern.

With the arrival of a mysterious telegram declaring merely "arriving tomorrow," the film cuts directly to a party connected with the arrival of the guest, who is given no name. The dingy sepia tones utilized in the brief limning of the family are transfused now with color, and the extreme perspectival structure of the frames yields to a more natural composition de-emphasizing geometrical depth when the stranger comes from a doorframe toward the camera. The use of color and non-depth composition is accompanied by an alteration in the family's behavior from mechanical plodding to effusive and natural expression. It seems clear that what Pasolini has done stylistically is to associate geometrical symmetry with rational power.

The idea of surfacity is appropriate to the stranger, for in every way he *is* his appearance. He seems, in fact, to be the "character" correlative of surface consciousness, one whose appearance is his substance; one who, as his lack of name suggests, does not possess the traditional impermeable identity we have come to associate with great art (as in the Lear of Shakespeare, the David Copperfield of Dickens, or even the unified narrative voice of a Hemingway hero). The stranger hardly has any voice at all. His primary organ of social relationship is his eye, not his mouth. He is a man without a past and thus without the determining indexes of inheritance, a man who lives fully within the moment. His future is as vague as his past. He manifests no psychological hang-ups and, indeed, is free to give himself sexually to each member of the family. He proffers no verbal advice, no instructions on living, and dispenses no intellectual wisdom. Is he controlled by a higher power? There is no evidence that his telegram is not sent by him nor that his departure is other than a decision of his own. His presence, his existence, remains mysterious in terms of the rational assumptions integral to the world he disrupts.

Constrained neither by fixed identity nor social mores, he is totally open to relationships with each member of the family, able to give the love demanded by each person, including the maid. This supple responsiveness to those around him reveals itself in his assimilation of each family member's own interests or occupation. He delves into the father's text on civil engineering, the mother's poetry books, the daughter's photographic displays, and the son's passion for the paintings of Francis Bacon. Clearly, one feature of this new spiritual consciousness is its harmonic adaptability to its environment; it is not in conflict with the cosmos. The Marxist facet of this harmony is the lack of age or class distinctions in the stranger's relationships. He moves easily from the maid to the family head, from playing soccer with Pietro and his friends to becoming the Father Confessor to the parents. His behavior is more Marxist than that of the most radical Marxist in its total abdication of abstract class distinctions between people. Thus, although the stranger's demeanor is verbally shallow, he is not without a sense of compassion and love.

As he avoids relating to others in terms of an imposed social position, so he is not defined in terms of a fixed social relationship outside himself. He comports himself with a disturbing self-containment which might easily be construed as passivity. For example, he does not actually initiate any of the sexual contacts with other family members; he imposes no will upon them at all, yet responds freely. Unburdened from the self-consciousness of a fixed identity, he is free from the impulse to possess and control, impulses Pasolini clearly identifies with the old bourgeois rationality through the speech of Paolo:

You have utterly destroyed the image I've always had of myself. Now I am unable to conceive of anything that could make me regain my identity. What do you suggest . . . social death? Total obliteration of myself? How could this be done by a man committed to the concepts of order, foresight, and above all possession?

The visitor, in keeping with his nature, responds with no rhetorical balm to this question. His wisdom is entirely contained in the nature of his life. But the questions raised by the industrialist reveal the flaw in his consciousness, for they imagine solutions only in terms of death or destruction, instead of self-creation.

As a definitive quality of bourgeois industrial consciousness, this obsession with the rational order of things is mirrored in Pasolini's use of extreme perspective. Whenever this world is shown, it seems almost to bind itself into the rigid physique of perspectival structure; whenever people try to behave feelingly or irrationally, the perspective fades. These associations are all the more clear when *Teorema* and *Medea* are viewed as companion pieces, for clearly in *Medea* the rise of a bourgeois middle class is shown to be intimately tied up with the emergence of rational (as opposed to mythical) consciousness and with the abstraction of space into depth-of-field geometrical constructions. In *Teorema* Pasolini looks at the historical end of this same bourgeois mentality and suggests that this end, while inevitable in light of bourgeois rationalism's exclusion of spiritual perception, is precipitated by the reappearance of a kind of spiritual force in the world. However, that vision is no longer bound to the rituals and symbols of Medea's world, but has transcended ritual entirely, just as it transcends rationality. The stranger who is the bearer of the new vision is free from conventional restraints, neither compelled to placate nature in ritual nor to dominate it.

Pasolini's concern with surfacity is evident in the interests of the household members, the personality of the visitor, and the style of the photography. Pietro is interested in painting; he even leaves home to pursue his interest, his choice of medium being opaque sheets of plastic. Odetta is a photographer who shares her work with the visitor. Emilia, the maid, is consumed with her own image, which she resurfaces at the end of the film. Conversely, Dad tries to find freedom by stripping away a surface, his clothing, the exterior trappings of civilization; and Lucia, his wife, will try, after the departure of the stranger, to recapture the experience of his presence by picking up young men who bear a surface resemblance to him.

The most elaborate surface involvement on the part of the household is a psychological one composed of each member's unconscious use of the visitor as a screen upon which to project his or her latent, previously unawakened, emotional needs. The stranger's physical appearance actually lends itself to this somewhat perverse use of itself. His perpetual white clothing, the fact that "he is often surrounded by sun or light,"[8] coupled with his implacable demeanor, endow him with something akin to a meta-cinematic embodiment of cinema, a surface bearing fictive possibilities. However, it is really the inability of the various household members to perceive him as such, which prompts their own dissolutions.

The Bourgeois Family's Responses to the Visitor

Through his rather passive and ego-less responsiveness—rather than through any active effort on his part—the visitor is endowed by each family member with the power of spiritual panacea. Each tries to possess him as an image of his or her own longed-for life consciousness. He evokes, really through the profound harmony of his self-containment, the loneliness and sense of insufficiency of each person in the house. Unable to assimilate his life force into his or her own consciousness, each figure makes the visitor into a static symbol of his own submerged sense of life. They become dependent on him and thus try to pressure him into playing the static, predictable role of lover, friend, and confidant. They are unable to move past the barrier of their bourgeois inheritance which equates love with possession and sanctions the process of relating to others as extensions of oneself. To carry out the analogy with the perspectival organization of their world, the visitor becomes the perspectival origin, the organizing point of reference for their lives. They sense the insufficiency of their old assumptions (as in the previously quoted speech of Dad) in dealing with the visitor, but never make the leap because they cannot conceive themselves in terms of what he is. It is the dilemma of Pasolini's Oedipus, who, despite the admonitions of the Sphinx about their kinship, never comprehends that the Sphinx is himself. The stranger's departure brings in its wake the spiritual drowning of each family member as well as that of the maid. To clarify the failure of surface consciousness these breakdowns involve (a failure, it must be recalled, which in simple terms is a refusal to locate spirit within oneself), Pasolini makes the postpartum life of each person center upon surfaces.

Odetta's particular instincts have always been to fix the visitor through the agency of her hobby, still photography. After seducing him over her collection of photographs, she takes a number of shots of him seated in the yard with her father. After the visitor's departure, she uses these photographs to recapture his presence in the yard. Her operation insists upon the sort of spatial depth to things which the visitor's advent has mitigated.

Odetta's possessive use of surfaces has been a facet of her life all along. In her first appearance in the film, she is discovered at school carrying a photograph of her father, which reveals either the Freudian nature of her particular problem or the compatibility of that neurosis with a larger context, the general loss of the power of the imagination to conceive of the possibility of the individuated consciousness unsupported by parental or social pinnings.

Her desire to fix relationships, when frustrated, turns upon itself to become self-fixation. In a scene which captures, as well as any I have seen, the sense of spiritual lassitude and exhaustion which accompanies an impending mental breakdown, Odetta aimlessly wanders about her house. She goes as far as the front gate to check the possible return of the visitor. She cannot actually leave the citadel of the home. She takes out the photographs and slowly walks about in a circle, staring at the camera, a sort of gesture of uncomprehension as to the immanent filmic nature of things. Finally, she lies down in the imperturbable paralysis of a catatonic trance. The failure to go forward becomes total fixity.

Prior to Odetta's paralysis, the maid Emilia departs for her rural hometown. In some respects, her experience is the most positive of the group, for she returns to an essentially religious primitive world and performs a miracle. Ironically, that achievement is the healing of sores on the face of a small boy, a triumph of surface functioning. Emilia herself is not transfigured by her experience, but ages rapidly, longing for the presence of the departed visitor. Like Odetta, she becomes increasingly immobile (sanctified in the peasant mind by her long, enduring stasis) and finally negates the self-image with which she has been concerned (for she is the most habituated to examining her countenance in mirrors) by covering herself with a layer of dirt in an excavation site. Her relation to surface, then, to some degree parallels her relation to the visitor, as it centered on her self-rejection and desire to live through another. The viewer may recall that Emilia's initial response to the visitor was an attempted suicide.

The moral delinquency of her return to the farm is underscored by the stylistic resumption of perspectival frame composition with her departure. As she waits for a tram, she is photographed with a wide-angle lens, which casts the street into the shape of a deep, linear corridor. After the spaciousness associated with the visitor (many of his scenes are shot in the open outdoors), the return of the perspectival shot seems positively constricting. As the camera tags along with Emilia, the sense of confinement increases. The bus station has a corridor line to it (we occasionally even see the outline of the original factory in the background), and when she leaves the bus, she enters a totally enclosed courtyard. The camera tracks in behind her, emphasizing the perspectival lines. In every way she seems decided to negate her own generative potential despite the healing powers she evinces. All of her actions deny contact with the world: she refuses food (except for nettles), refuses personal contact, and dedicates herself to suffering. All that remains of her at film's end is her eyes (for they are the only part left uncovered by the dirt in the excavation site), now transformed into organs of self-pity. They can only cry, refusing the light of the world disclosed in the figure of the visitor.

Like Emilia, the other family members insist upon the presence of the visitor as an externalized symbol to give meaning to their lives. Their symbol-bound perception is underscored, in fact, when they replace Emilia with a maid who resembles her and whom they address with the same name. People clearly exist here as functional icons, the sterile robots of a codified reality. Ironically, Emilia, herself, is converted by the peasants into an externalized icon of spirituality.

Pietro's foundering in life is even more closely associated with the perversion of surface than Emilia's. He leaves the secure womb of his family to live out his artistic ambition to paint. Like that of Emilia, his departure becomes a journey into ever greater enclosure and perspectival sovereignty. His little garret (itself a perfect model of bourgeoisness) is located in a dead-end street.

Emilia resurfacing herself [from Teorama]

As with Odetta, Pietro reveals his true passion for painting to be an attempt to recover a sense of the visitor's presence. He tries to find a shade of blue which will match the blue of the visitor's eyes. Unable to do this, and unable to live with his isolation, he manufactures a way to obliterate himself through art: "I must try to devise new techniques that will be unrecognizable, unlike anything that has ever been done before, to avoid childish ridicule, to build a world of my own, a world not comparable to anything, a world that isn't subject to existing sets of values . . . no one must realize its creator is worthless." What he proceeds to do, compatible with the linearity Pasolini associates stylistically with rational consciousness, is cover transparent plastic sheets with lines. He stacks these one on top of another until his cinematic image is obliterated. His art, thus, is merely a means of hiding from the challenge of individuality, not a tool of individuation.

This whole operation, then, is revealed as an exercise in self-obliteration—cinematically, the negation of the powers of the image so potently embodied by the visitor. In fact, there is a strong element of irony in all of this which makes it a parody of individuation. In his impassioned speech to the departing visitor, Pietro had exclaimed: "I don't recognize myself. All I had in common with others has been destroyed. I was like everyone else; I had many faults, my own and those I acquired. You've made me different; severed me from the natural order of things." While part of the effect of the visitor is the provocation of self-awareness in each of the household members, none is able to grow beyond it. While they set out immediately into more enterprising modes of individual action, the tone is deceptive; the modes are merely retreats from life in disguise.

Like her son, Luccia is induced into the experience of painful self-awareness: "My emptiness was filled with false and petty values. . . . Now I'm aware of it." And like him, she retreats to familiar territory, ultimately enclosing herself in the dark spaces of a country church after unsatisfying sexual encounters with young men who vaguely resemble the visitor. Her breakdown reveals another dimension of the structure of bourgeois consciousness: the familiar spirit/flesh dualism so prevalent in a film like *Accatone*. As Luccia's sexual urges become more frantic, the presence of traditional religious structures becomes more obvious in the background—a church one time, a monastery another time. Her sexual and religious cravings, once appeasable through the visitor, are totally sundered, for she now pursues one at the cost of the other. Religion becomes available only in institutionalized forms (hence the

Shazaman sleeps below the copper man [*Arabian Nights*]

churches), sex in figures with no emotional sensitivity (one pickup practically rapes her in a ditch). This divorce of instincts into irreconcilable
camps reveals, finally, the latent fragmentation of consciousness upon
which the bourgeois mind is founded.

The family's spiritual failures have uncovered roughly four aspects of
fracture in the bourgeois life: the iconography of people, the severance
of art from life, the repressed emotional life of familial ties, and the
disjunction of spirit and flesh. It is Paolo (in whom these problems are
conjoined) who attempts to heal the disease by casting off civilization
itself, the perceived source of the problems. He first divests himself of
the personal trappings of culture, his clothes; then the public raiments,
i.e., the city, by retreating to a primitive desert (near an extinct volcano).
It is appropriate that his peregrinations from a train terminal (shot with
a radical insistence on perspective) end in a place so devoid of human
imprint, for he has, in essence, regressed from the challenge of surfacity
into an unworkable primitivism.

The deficiency of the bourgeois response, in light of the life possibilities generated by the Stamp character, is underscored as well by the
continuation of color in the film even after his departure. The inability
of the characters to see the change is an index of their personal failure
rather than that of Stamp or of the world. In Pasolini's jargon, the mundane has been revealed as divine and the condition does not alter with
the loss of the visitor. Likewise, if the world of the characters becomes
more perspectively rigid, it is because they refuse to see in any other
way.

The Factory

The problem of individuality in *Teorema* is obviously that of the
inability of the individual to find enough value within himself to make
living worthwhile. By this, the film does not advocate monastic isolation
for everyone nor deny the need for relationships; like most Pasolini films,
it implies at its core that only those persons capable of sensing that isolation and not fleeing it can be capable of fuller life. But in most cases,
as people are stripped of old forms of organization and thrown upon
their own resources, they experience only confusion. This process may
explain the activity in the opening scenes.

The first episode occurs prior to the credits, at an industrial plant, but
is, in actuality, the aftermath of the story which follows it. A company
lawyer is besieged by reporters on the grounds of a factory which has
just been turned over to its workers. The discussion between the lawyer

and the reporters reveals Pasolini's cynicism in regard to both the bourgeois donor and the "Marxist" revolutionaries who, presumably, stand to be the beneficiaries of the bequest. According to the reporters, the donation will not only fail to benefit the previous owner but, more significantly, will merely transform the workers into the very bourgeoisie against whom they have been struggling. Workers, reporters, and lawyers welter in a state of confusion, and one cannot help but feel that the situation expresses Pasolini's vision of the logical result of a worker's revolution in which the consciousness of the proletariat has been conditioned by their dependence upon the organizing stimulus of the bourgeoisie. Because of their inherent materialism, the goal they seek can only transform them into the "enemy." Dialectical materialism ends by transforming everyone into a materialist, failing, in the process, to achieve a holistic vision of life with which, in Pasolini's mind, the revolution once pulsed. They are as unable to deal with irrational change as the family whose story follows because their minds, like those of the bourgeoisie, are bound to the necessity of class definitions and categorical struggles to define their lives. Hence, as the scene ends, one revolutionary exclaims, "If the bourgeoisie changes, if it achieves the transformation of all people into a middle class, there is no room for class struggle."

While the mentality of the workers has been conditioned to believe in the eternal necessity of conflict in life, Pasolini has portrayed, in the person of the visitor, a life-style free of conflict. Attraction, love, and convergence are the principles revealed in his relationships, contacts with individuals free from the urge to possess or control. This radical vision of human freedom, with its air of complete noncompromise, is profoundly typical of Pasolini the social renegade, and is almost inevitable in his work from its inception.

9

Pigsty: Predation and Consumer Society

PIGSTY IS, despite Pasolini's distaste for ideological films,[1] his one feature-length work which is undeniably political. Its concerns, in fact, are not necessarily embedded in the structure. One portion of the film is almost entirely verbal and conceptual, a condition partly attributable to Pasolini's short-lived interest in the theater (*Pigsty* was written as a play rather than a film). Its filming resulted from the author's sudden theoretical reversal, "elevating" theater, semiologically, to the status of cinema. Fortunately, this confusion in media was temporary. *Pigsty,* for most Pasolini fans, is the least interesting of his works, an attitude largely merited by the allegory and verbality of the film.

The film is constructed narratively on the montage principle of collision. Two stories, separated in time and having almost no shared literal context, are intercut and thus juxtaposed. Thematically, each deals with a vision of man as a predator who devours and is devoured by other men and animals. Each in some way embodies the issues and processes of the other.

The first story pictures a largely Marxist view of human history in which man rises as a predator from feeding on animals to feeding on other men. A naked, bestial man in a barren desert kills a butterfly, tries to eat it, and convulses. He moves on to snakes and plants with slightly better results. Presently he encounters the remains of some medieval armor from a battle and dons it; moving on in the desert, he meets up with a column of soldiers. One drops behind and the original character attacks and kills him, then cannibalizes the body after severing the head and tossing it into a chasm. As his cannibalism continues, this last act becomes, through repetition, a religious rite. He gathers a group of cannibals about him, but they are eventually captured by an army under the aegis of the church. While his companions repent, the protagonist remains unregenerate; his only words are, "I killed my father, I have

121

eaten human flesh, and I tremble with joy." The group is staked out to
be eaten by dogs.

In its contours this story presents, to a degree, a Marxist view of economic history insofar as it depicts that history as a process of predatory
dialectic. The introduction of tools and civilization into the primitive
world of the protagonist serves to facilitate the transfer of his predatory
drives from animals to men. The tools, in fact, guns and swords, are
designed specifically for that end, the products of a society used to prey-
ing on other men. That our protagonist immediately knows their use
reinforces the sense of historical imperative in the process. Yet while the
cannibalism unfolds, one is always aware that its source lies in one of the
conditions of life: hunger. The fact is, the protagonist must eat, and if
he, in turn, is eaten we must see the social system as an extension of the
personal instinct for survival.

The second story involves a German industrialist named Glotz—who
closely resembles Hitler; his son, Julian; and a rival, Herdhitze. Herdhitze and Glotz, through their inchoate plans to eliminate each other,
have discovered that each is a former Nazi. Moreover, Herdhitze has
learned from his private investigators that Glotz's son is capable of having erotic relations only with swine. This weakness seems part and parcel
of Julian's general paralysis (he lies in a coma for part of the film), the
cause of which is his inability to throw off his father's inheritance of Nazi
capitalism. He is half revolutionary and half conformist to his father's
way of life so that, in Pasolini's phrase, "he is nothing."[2] We learn at
film's end that he has been eaten by the pigs even as his father and
Herdhitze were reestablishing their former partnership. The coordina-
tion of the two actions seems almost causal rather than coincidental.

Consumption

The one motif which clearly unites the narrative threads is that of
"eating."[3] The opening words of the film written on tombstones
announce, "For your disobedience we have devoured you," and the
opening shots of the film proper show the protagonist eating a butterfly,
then a snake, and then other humans. Only once does sexual lust enter
into the first narrative, and its power as a motivating force is secondary
to that of the need to eat. Hunger is clearly the historical matrix out of
which the conditions in part two of the film arise. In this case, however,
the hunger of the stomach has reached fulfillment in a psychological
obsession, the fanatic urge for consumption *en masse*, be it in the form

of devouring entire races (the Jews, to whom Herdhitze drinks), or in the creation of a consumer society in which predatory instincts are fostered and exploited rather than transformed into creative energy. Hence, Julian, the "product" of this society, suffers from arrested growth and the inability to do anything but die. His father's need for a wheelchair manifests the paralysis inherent in the predatory system, the real inheritance passed on from father to son.

While the capitalists are engaged in consumption (of Jews, beer, factories), the revolutionary youth seems obsessed with its opposite: elimination. Julian's girl friend speaks of the youth of Germany "pissing" on the Berlin Wall, an action whose symbolic rebellion exceeds its functional value. They share a dislike of the old system, but lack a clear idea of what a new one might consist of. They are the bourgeois students whom Pasolini criticized in 1968.

Carried to its extreme, consumption merely becomes a form of elimination, suggested not only by the students' urination but by the capitalist process itself. Herdhitze has saved himself from a trial for war crimes by carefully destroying all evidence of the bodies he killed for research (they were totally "consumed" by fire). Consumption in its raw form is envisioned as a mask for the will to annihilate. Appropriately, at film's end, with the death of Julian, Herdhitze will advise the peasants who inform him of the death that if no trace of the body can be found, then one can blithely ignore the death as though it never happened. Morality requires social consensus, not personal conscience, for the capitalist. Perfect consumption equals perfect justice.

Another common element in the two narratives involves the use of the human head in a symbolic function. Herdhitze, we learn, seems to have had a particular fascination with human skulls. His activities involved killing people to better "study" their heads. By comparison, the primitive protagonist of the first narrative performs a ritual act with each murder; he severs the victim's head and throws it in a volcanic pit, a pit whose belching smoke associates it with the industrial world of Herdhitze's Germany. Both models of action strongly imply an attack upon the seat of intelligence, literally, the head. Each figure remains controlled by the physical urge for consumption to the point of abnegating the seat of mental power by which he might grow beyond his animalistic, predatory existence.

The narrative development of the film begins with an act of consumption based on simple hunger and ends with the concealment of an act of consumption which has resulted from a neurotic obsession rather than from physical imperative. The obsession with the body destroys the mind; the possibilities for greater life are thwarted.

The issue of concealment has ramifications along at least two other lines in the film. Herdhitze has undergone a facelift: "Plastic surgery is advanced in Italy," notes Glotz, with an irony revealing Pasolini's vision of the political trend in Italy. The disguises worn by the industrialists foster the need for more subtle detection methods to determine the nature of one's identity. Each has hired private detectives to discover the identity of his antagonist. Metaphysically, the quest for economic supremacy becomes a rational game, dividing the world into appearance and reality, illusion and essence. In this case, of course, the outward image matches the inner, predatory reality; but, as a comment on fascism, the division of appearance and reality becomes a trademark of the Fascist mode of operation. Founded on a lie, that individuality is personal fascism, it must conceal the absurdity of its condition.

This problem arising from the ambiguity of appearances is carried over in the person of Julian to a problem of ambiguous identity. Julian seems to be only an extension of the ways others choose to view him, as in the dialogue between his mother and his girl friend:

MOTHER: He never went back on decisions.
GIRL FRIEND: He never made any!
MOTHER: He wasn't intelligent but attached to ideas.
GIRL FRIEND: I never knew a boy as bright.
. . . .
MOTHER: He didn't like to travel.
GIRL FRIEND: He always thought of distant people.

This ambiguity of character in Julian reminds one of the Terence Stamp character in *Teorema*, but unlike the stranger, Julian lacks the plasticity of change and the ability to generate changes in those about him. His obscurity of self leads, thematically, to his complete disappearance from the film, a disappearance we are not allowed to witness but learn of secondhand from the peasants.

Julian's own mental problems involve his inability to attach his affections to human beings. Controlled by his attraction to swine (another model of the failure to grow beyond animal drives), he becomes absorbed by them. The old saw about the sow that eats its piglets hangs like the scent of bad breath over the film.

The pigsty in which Julian disappears provides another link between the two principal narratives, for not only is it tended by Ninetto Davoli, who appears also in the first "cannibal" narrative, but its very shape, as we see it at the beginning of the film, consisting of bleak, regimented stalls, reminds one of the photographs of Nazi concentration camps, like those, for instance, in Alain Resnais' *Night and Fog*. The predatory drives of man, the hungry animal, are thus associated with their extension, the predation and atrocities of fascism.

One also recognizes in the narrative an obvious division between that portion of the story which relies on words (modern Cologne) and that which relies on images (the cannibals). However, unlike his work in *The Hawks and the Sparrows*, Pasolini's division of the narrative scenes is less metaphysical—less a conflict of word and image—than dramatic: a means of juxtaposing man the physical beast with man the verbal capitalist. There is little difference; language merely provides a convenient cosmetic mask for the social blemishes wrought by Herdhitze, Glotz, and company.

The one use of language in the story of the cannibals occurs at the end of that narrative. The protagonist, while being tied to the stake, unregeneratively asserts, "I have killed my father, eaten human flesh and I tremble with joy." This is consumption at its most outrageous, the natural conclusion to Oedipal instincts, which could lead one to conclude that Pasolini's vision of history is founded on father-son conflicts. Indeed, he partially confirms this at times, though not in a strictly Freudian sense. In addition, one almost hears in this an echo of the sacrament of the Roman Catholic Mass. The possibility is latently present in the repeated dialogue involving the issue of the "obedient son." The voices of Glotz and his wife Bertha are heard over the images at the film's beginning, discussing the obediency of Julian; Julian's relationship with his father is also the concern of his girl friend. The issue of obediency has a submerged Oedipal (or Freudian) dimension insofar as it is Julian's subservience to his father which has in part produced his problems. Pasolini envisions a little Oedipal aggression as necessary to liberate Julian from his paralysis, to free one generation from its predecessors. However, our view of this must be modified by the cannibal's last phrase, an unmitigated celebration of Oedipal instincts which serve only the ends of predation. Oedipal rebellion can be a form of growth or one of the pillars of capitalist society. Frankly, Freud seems reduced to a contradiction.[4]

In this manner, Pasolini deprives us of easy explanations or solutions to the problem, but that solution, in whatever forms it will take, must clearly be a departure from the traditional religious, psychological, or political answers. That the film itself provides no solution, other than by implication in its presentation of negative models, is a limitation of the work rather than the pessimism of the author. As he explores the topic in "The Trilogy of Life," new possibilities, at least, begin to emerge.

10

The Decameron: The Sexual Frame

THE DECAMERON is the first film in a series which Pasolini dubbed his "Trilogy of Life." Each film in the trilogy is inspired by an earlier collection of stories (Boccaccio's *Il Decameron*, Chaucer's *The Canterbury Tales*, and the anonymous *The Thousand and One Nights*) in which narration itself assumes a self-conscious importance. Pasolini has capitalized (pardon the expression) on the self-reflective quality of these works to deepen the germinal notions developed in *Teorema* that medium entails content: "I must say that these last ones of the trilogy of life . . . represent a fascinating and marvellous experience . . . this experience of entering into the most mysterious workings of artistic creation, this proceeding into the ontology of narration, in making of cinema, cinema . . . I find it the most beautiful idea I have ever had, this wish to recount, for the sheer joy of telling and recounting the creation of narrative myths, away from ideology. . . ."[1]

In actuality, there is a great deal pertaining to ideology within the films in the trilogy. In fact, these films, even more explicitly than those of the earlier trilogy, contain a history of the rise of the middle class, its mutually exploitative relationship with organized religion, and its impulse to indenture the artist or otherwise mitigate his powers of imagination. But since ideological preponderance also withers the imagination (e.g., in *Pigsty*), Pasolini has buried his political interests within the trilogy as a function of the narrative process and the artistic issues. He complains of his critics, in fact, that they are insensitive to the formal aspects of his work and tend to look for overt political diatribe: "The younger generations . . . have become, for example, a-critical with regard to form, because they no longer sense formal problems, having been brutalized by a series of horrible forms, and thus lost the sense of beauty, of aesthetics of achieved completeness. . . ."[2]

After the ideological orgy of *Pigsty*, Pasolini, in the same interview,

129

Pasolini, the creator, playing the role of the artist Giotto turns toward his "idealized" fresco in The Decameron recommits his art to life in its concreteness rather than to ideology: "I think the only thing one can hope for is the creation of a series of relationships with an ever-increasing number of individuals. Not groups. I do not believe in working in a decidedly social, mundane, organized way. . . . Since my vocation is literary and artistic and thus beyond being simply ideological or political . . . I believe very much in the concreteness of things."[3]

When juxtaposed to his intrigue with narration, his affirmation of concreteness in this trilogy leads to a rather explicit vision of existence as a narrative act, of man as a creature who becomes what his imagination is capable of narrating. Hence, within the "Trilogy of Life," artistic creation is ideally an activity not divorced from life, nor a diversion from a more important concern, but a process which *is* life. Consequently, each film is presided over by an artist figure, and we can measure the conditions of spiritual health in these films by assessing the degree of integration achieved by the artists with the life of the concrete world. In only one of the films, *The Arabian Nights*, does artistic imagination achieve a full marriage with life and in only this film is life pictured as being tolerable, neither the cesspool whose metaphor dominates *The Decameron* nor the excretory hell with which *The Canterbury Tales* ends, but a world of creative relationships between an "increasing number of individuals."

The organization of the three films in the "Trilogy of Life" roughly parallels that of the *Oedipus/Medea/Teorema* group in its transition from physical to rational to visual emphasis in its history of consciousness. Hence, while sexual (physical) hunger prevails in *The Decameron* as the prime source of exploitation, monetary power drives most of the characters of *The Canterbury Tales*, and self-liberation impels the protagonists of *The Arabian Nights*. Thus the films progress in a sort of hierarchy from the life of the body to the life of the mind (profit becoming a virtually incorporeal obsession) to the life and liberation of a holistic imagination.

On a more microcosmic level, this trinary matrix of body/intellect/imagination also enters the configuration of each film with a series of metaphoric associations. Because it is a way of visual experience, holistic imagination takes for its particular agent the organs of vision and their medium, images; the powers of the intellect are associated with words, the comprehension of abstractions, and, symbolically, the head; and the life of the body is associated with sexuality, instinct, and, symbolically, the hand. While these associations are obviously overreductive and schematic, they can serve as guideposts to the nature of change transpiring in the films. Thus, for example, the fact that *The Decameron* can be quite neatly split at its midway point to disclose the kinship of all episodes on one side with verbal narration, and the kinship of the others with images and visions, strongly suggests that Pasolini is dealing with a series of life situations in which man's verbal/intellectual powers are sundered from his imaginative, creative energies. In fact, what occurs in the film is not only the disjunction of these facets of man but their steplike vitiation through the inability of the people either to comprehend their lives intellectually or to imagine themselves as more than a physical event. These processes are further complicated by being interwoven with the rise and development of the middle class, institutionalized religion, secular philosophy and art, and the role of the artist in society. Each film opens with an artist figure mired in a marketplace.

If one wants a more immediately relevant and down-to-earth handle with which to explore the trilogy, the one human experience common to each film, and even to each episode, is the quest for love; the films, however, also document the pressures which destroy it. For the most part, love is confused by the characters of *The Decameron* with sexual gratification or spiritual purity. If not this, then it is used as an enticement (by, for example, the three women in the first major episode) to entrap and swindle the unsuspecting. The figures in *The Canterbury Tales* tend to replace it with love of profit or of power; and only in *The Arabian Nights* is it fully realized.

Correlative to their concerns with love, each film is inhabited by overt artist figures whose relationship to life and the trinary model of holism forms an index of the capacity of love to flourish in the world. In the first two films we see artists who, reflecting the desolation in their societies, become progressively separated from their subject matter and from life. In the third film we are presented with an artist whose material is her life, a celebration of liberation and love.

The trinary model which sustains the structuring of these films does not exclude man's psychological life from consideration but provides a differentiating index for it. There is a sense, however, that character, self, and psychology are no longer the real subjects for scrutiny, that, in fact, since *Teorema*, they are nugatory illusions or subjects already exhausted by Pasolini to his own satisfaction.

The Narrative Progress of *The Decameron*

Pasolini's movement beyond character as subject matter is revealed in *The Decameron* by the absence of a central protagonist. Instead, we have a series of episodes which derives its cohesiveness from the interrelationship of the stories, as does, for example, a "novel" like Joyce's *Dubliners*. The absence of a protagonist is also compensated for by the recurring presence of two figures, Franco Citti as the character Ciappelletto and Pasolini himself as the painter Giotto,[4] who serve independently to tie certain episodes together by "framing" them. Their own episodes throw a frame around other stories in the film by which the film is divided in two, as shown below.[5]

PART ONE   *Ciappelletto*/Andreuccio/*Ciappelletto*/Masetto
            Peronella/*Ciappelletto*
PART TWO   *Giotto*/Riccardo/*Giotto*/Lorenzo/Don Gioni/Tingoccio/
            Giotto

The emphasis on frames and framing created by this structure is integrally involved with the issues in the episodes. For example, Giotto must employ frames as limits to his work. More nebulously, other people frame each other through deception or coercion; Riccardo, for instance, will be framed—coerced—though willingly, into marrying Isabetta.

But before probing these issues, we may note that the bisection of the movie suggested by the framing reveals other general trends. The Ciappelletto episodes, as they begin with his assault on a body and end with a deification of his own corpse, proclaim the destruction of corporeality as one process germane to that half of the film, a demolition somehow in league with self-delusion. (For example, Ciappelletto is sanctified because a ridiculously absurd confession he makes on his deathbed is taken by a priest as the truth.) In the second half of the film, the prominence of a painter, a man working with images, coupled with his failure to complete his project, suggests that artistic imagination is under attack in this portion of the film, in some way eroded by its encloser in a system of formalized religion which, through its otherworldliness, undermines the natural course of creative inclination.

Let us, then, consider the opening scene of the first portion of the movie. Ciappelletto appears in a medium close-up, frontal shot, beating someone to death. Before being ground into unconsciousness, the victim (who remains unseen) cries out, "You have understood nothing!"[6] Ciappelletto next appears carrying a heavy bundle through some narrow streets in the deepening twilight. He drops the loaded sack off a cliff and spits after it.

The shadow of this murder more or less looms over its companion episodes, for, like it, they are all concerned with the misuse of the body and, likewise, with a failure to understand. This probability is born out immediately as the Ciappelletto episode is succeeded by the story of Andreuccio, the son of a middle-class merchant, who is duped by some clever and unscrupulous women.

The problem of a breakdown in man's power of comprehension is introduced promptly by the relative ease with which Andreuccio is deceived into believing one of the women is his long-lost sister. His sort of intellectual innocence (reminiscent of Pasolini's Oedipus) leads him to weltering in a cesspool. Once divested of his clothes (which hold his money), he is fed a laxative (which he imbibes with innocent simple-mindedness), and, feeling an attack on his bowels, runs into a commode whose floorboards have been deliberately weakened. As usual, innocence has no value in Pasolini's vision of things and Andreuccio takes a dive into "experience."

While befoulment intrudes thematically through Andreuccio's stupidity, it also inheres in the misuse of language, for it is by verbal deception that Andreuccio is entrapped. That is, if intellect is deficient, its primary tool, language, suffers a corruption. Hence the use of words, for mischievous deception becomes a common factor in all of the Ciappelletto-framed stories.

But Andreuccio's episode is not finished. He climbs from the cistern and runs to the outskirts of town, where he encounters two grave-robbers who feed him another story, convincing him to crawl inside an occupied casket and rob the corpse. Andreuccio complies, this time trying to work a little deception of his own. He lies to his accomplices that the sought-for ruby is gone; they retaliate by closing the lid upon him. Andreuccio has moved from being a total innocent, to being a twice-duped fool, to being a self-duped fool prevaricating like his tormentors. He is saved only by the arrival of other grave-robbers, who subsequently flee when bitten on the leg by Andreuccio. Cinematically, Andreuccio never makes it out of the tomb. He is last seen still standing in freeze frame by the wan light of the doorway, holding his ruby while covered in excrement. What he has learned to comprehend is how to lie, hence to debase the mouth, its most helpful function being deception for the sake of profit. Also, the reference to corporeality, in the violation of the bishop's remains, implies that the misuse of the flesh will be sustained as an issue in the film.

The close of Andreuccio's episode opens upon a second appearance of Ciappelletto in which the misuse of language, especially narrative language, is clearly dramatized. A crowd of people has gathered about a man reading the tale of Massetto in the nunnery (which ensues in the film) from a copy of Boccaccio's *Il Decameron*. Captivated by the words of the story, the listeners no longer pay attention to the incidents in their immediate sphere of perception. While their eyes are settled upon the imaginary reality of the story, Ciappelletto carefully picks their pockets. He then uses his booty to purchase carnal pleasures from a young man standing warily on the periphery of the action. The element of prostitution (with which Franco Citti is perpetually associated, alas) becomes an aspect of the linguistic debasement at hand; literally, word power is exploited for profit, and the profit used to buy flesh, the process being engendered by obsession with corporeity.

In the Masetto episode which follows, words fare little better, becoming the victims of a disembodied spirituality seeking to construct a bridge back to the physical world. As with Ciappelletto, words become coins with which to secure sexual satiety. Masetto starts the process through a scheme to gain access to some nunnery inmates who, he assumes correctly, are sexually starved. He exploits the communal honor of speech by pretending to be dumb (loss of words being equated with loss of testicles by the mother superior). His scheme, engendered as a fantasy of unlimited carnal indulgence, backfires when his prodigious activity in the nunnery drains his energy. He is thus moved to complain, but his verbal eruption does not destroy his game, it merely prompts the mother superior to proclaim his speech a miracle, thus procuring his stud service permanently. All of the equivocation builds a bridge of lies between the life of the spirit and the life of the flesh, which are inevitably separated by the very nature of the nunnery. The two are allowed to coexist, but under a pretense which does not erase the dualism germane to the sexual repression. As in the other episodes, verbal narration operates only as a function of sexual interest, for the "profit" of a system already psychically fragmented.

The perversion of narrative language pertinent to each of these episodes is emphasized by an increasing degree of "rot" in the mouths of the characters. Speech is decomposing; thus the mouth of the bursar (the most conspicuous man of profit in the Masetto episode) flashes a cave full of disgustingly stained teeth, and the mouth of Peronella's husband (in the episode following Masetto's) holds a grotesquely deformed ganglia of "tusks" which still, despite their repugnance, are not yet as fully repellent as those of the German merchants in the final episode of the first half of the film. Stained, corroded, and seemingly festering with the flotsam of the latrine in which Andreuccio floundered, their teeth wind from the gums like a clump of deracinated trees.

The decline of the mouth as a factotum to the pleasures of the flesh (metaphoric in the Ciappelletto and Masetto stories) becomes overt and literal in the Peronella episode, as we begin this story with the heroine administering oral sex to her boy friend. Their play is interrupted by the unexpected return of Peronella's husband with his face full of sharklike teeth. She outflanks any marital perturbation through a lie which transforms her lover into a pot buyer. She even inveigles her husband into cleaning the inside of a huge crock and, while his vision is obscured, engages in sexual intercourse with her lover. With this image of the husband enclosed within the crock we literally see the increasing narrowness of vision of those who are victimized by the perversion of narrative speech for sexual ends. One might say that art, as represented by the pottery, has become an agent of obfuscation rather than enlightenment, just as its verbal corollary, narration, has.

The decline of narration is consummated in the episode which concludes part one of the film, Ciappelletto's journey to Germany as a debt collector for a wealthy bourgeois merchant: a natural conclusion to the life experiences it follows. Preceded by a cinematic recreation of Peter Breughel's paintings, *The Triumph of Death* and *The Combat of Lent and Carnival*, his trip turns into his own funeral; but while the rotten-mouthed brothers, his intended victims, listen, Ciappelletto provides a priest with an outrageous series of confessional lies which parody the Seven Deadly Sins (gluttony becomes a lust for lettuce). He is sanctified and deserves it, say the brothers, for calling so much "profitable" attention to their house. Business will prosper, and thus the repressive forces of religion and capitalist profit, coupled primarily with the carnal obsessions of the people and their disdain for comprehension, result in an apotheosis of death—purveyed literally in the sanctifying of Ciappelletto's body. Carnality, even under the guise of religious approbation, is worshipped.

Before considering the episodes in the second half of the film, the viewer might note other connections between the episodes. Most of the main characters, for example, are middle-class merchants. Pasolini is clearly interested in the rise of that class, which he seems to see as being in league with the institutions of religion. They share an obsession with sex and corporeity, they both tend to remove themselves from the world—in the film they each occupy castles or houses ostensibly high (from Andreuccio's long drop to the street, to the cloud-capped nunnery and Peronella's upper-floored apartment)—and both debase verbal narrative for their own ends of profit. Also, considering those episodes in part one which exclude Ciappelletto, we find that each discloses an exploitation of men by women. Andreuccio is taken in by the collective plot of three women; Masetto becomes a captive of the sexual demands of the mother superior; and Peronella manages to exploit both males, boy friend and husband, using the husband to frighten the lover into purchasing a crock, using the lover to deceive the husband about her philandering. The ascension of femininity is portrayed as an aspect of carnal preoccupation.

This sundering of sexual relationships is one of several ruptures in the chain of events which originates in the divorce of body and mind. Moreover, the disruption of male-female relationships in the film infiltrates various levels of life: kinship, through Andreuccio's hoodwinking; marriage, in the Peronella story; and religion, in the Masetto episode. These rents in the fabric of life, within the historical context of the middle-class ascendancy, include all aspects of human relationships, each splitting into incompatible units which can be unified only through lies. The interplay of cause and effect in this process is, to say the least, tangled, but the general failures of life begin with a failure of consciousness, of imagination, or more relevantly of the ability to experience love. Whether this lack is fostered by middle-class ascension or merely a coexistent fact of life is not entirely clear; they seem mutually conditioning, and even inevitable, in the secular revolt of man from a repressive religion.

An index of the fracture in sexual relationships is the darkening mood of the film, purveyed in the progressive prevalence of somber tones. Excluding Ciappelletto's initial night scene, the episodes of the film are shot with ever lower lighting, ever darker hues, so that the crystal blue sky which characterizes the introduction of Andreuccio and Masetto is nearly absent in Ciappelletto's sojourn in Germany (and totally absent in the Tingoccio episode). The somberness, of course, is bolstered by Pasolini's emphasis on the trunk of human skulls in his tribute to Breughel. The skull provides an apt image for the conclusion of part one if for no other reason than its symbolic connotations of intellectual death. Thus, the injunction of Ciappelletto's first victim ("You have understood nothing") is transformed into a palpable image of desiccated mind, of the decomposition of the understanding faculties. With

The Decameron: Ciapelleto (Franco Citti) picks pockets while the people listen to Bocaccio telling tales
The Museum of Modern Art/Film Stills Archive

this death of mind, we proceed into part two of the film and the death of imagination.

The Second Half of the Film

If the process of the first half of the film engenders the deterioration of narrative speech, intellect, and comprehension, the second portion deals with the debasement of vision, either as imagination or as the integration of the eye with life. This debasement involves (more explicitly than in part one) a process of "framing," the enclosure of vision and imagistic thought in neat but restrictive parameters. Thus, as in the first half, the stories in part two are framed by episodes featuring one protagonist, in this case a painter (Giotto) played by Pasolini.

By the visual nature of his occupation, the painter's entrance into the film signals a shift in the narrative from its concern with words to a preoccupation with images. The decline of vision pertinent to this half of the film, like the demolition of intellect in the part one, results from the coupled forces of sexual obsession and middle-class materialism. In fact, as a lead-in to Pasolini's version of *The Canterbury Tales*, which is even more concerned with middle-class capitalism, this portion of *The Decameron* places greater emphasis on man's neurotic attachment to a social identity as a fundamental source of the misery in his world.

The second portion of the film is also more complicated than the first. It converts the binary problem, mind versus body, into a trinary event—mind/body/imagination—in which the latter power, explicitly embodied in a visual artist, fails to integrate the fragmented life energies into an operable whole.

One might construct a diagram which divulges the differing patterns between Parts One and Two:

PART ONE CIAPPELLETTO: verbal narrative/exploitation of men by women/body worship/mental death/verbal lies.

PART TWO GIOTTO: visual art/exploitation of women by men/framing of identity in social role/demise of imagination/separation of art and life/theatrical role-playing replaces verbal lying.

Part two opens with a shot of Giotto and a friend interrupting their journey to seek shelter from a rainstorm in a ramshackle hut. Inside the hut is a "looney" named Genarino. The painter trades his wet clothes for Genarino's dry ones and departs, laughing about his disguise. These

The Decameron: Worship of the skulls
The Museum of Modern Art/Film Stills Archive

simple events set the tone for the remainder of the film. The process of taking shelter becomes, in the context of the other episodes, a retreat from nature and an incarceration of life energies within unhealthy structures, hence the presence of the mentally deficient Genarino in the initial shelter (a vestige, perhaps, of the demise of intellection in part one). Strongly suggested by the episode (simple though it be) is a sense that the pursuit of security can become unhealthy. Moreover, the disguise of the artist—a sheltering of his self-image—not only extends this problem of disguise to self-obliteration but introduces, as well, another germ of dualism: the split between appearance and reality. By film's end this becomes essentially a process of creating an idealized appearance with which to cloak an unpleasant reality, a separation of art from life. Thus, in each of the two following episodes, the actions of the protagonists are predicated on the desire to improve their public appearance and social status for either sexual or monetary gain, and thus to negate their individuality.

Caterina and Riccardo are infatuated with each other. Caterina arranges to sleep on her balcony where Riccardo can visit her. In the morning they are discovered by her father while they are sleeping. Their bed is furnished with a curtain which frames it in such a way as to suggest its likeness to a stage. And, indeed, they are soon "theatrically" framed by Caterina's father. Instead of being outraged, he is delighted with his catch, for he recognizes Riccardo as the scion of a wealthy family. But he plays the role of outraged father, coercing Riccardo into marriage for the sake of monetary gain and social prestige. The scene ends with the curtains being closed (the end of the act) and Caterina and Riccardo "framed" on a parody stage. The voyeurism of Caterina's father (hence his powers of vision) is a means of increasing his social standing; the natural love of Caterina and Riccardo flourishes only insofar as it promotes the bourgeois goals of the parent.

The use of voyeurism is even more explicit in the story of Isabetta and Lorenzo. Their episode opens with her vulgar-looking brother (a degraded replacement for Caterina's father) spying upon their lovemaking. Because Lorenzo is merely an apprentice in the brother's business (there are three brothers), the eldest brother is outraged by the affair; he decides to murder Lorenzo. Lured to the woods by the theatrical machinations of the brothers, Lorenzo is duly killed and buried. But Isabetta (reflecting the already declining force of vision) is granted a vision of the specter of her dead lover. She finds his body, decapitates it, and places the head in a flower pot. The pot is then placed in her square window frame, the image which opened the episode. Thus Lorenzo is framed, literally, by the decapitation and, figuratively, by the brothers who kill him because of his lowly status. The powers of seeing are reduced to functions of social role-playing, and, as in the Riccardo/Caterina story, a love relationship, holistically unifying sexuality and spirituality, is marred by the perception of it in commercial terms. Lorenzo's decapitation implies that its cause, the obsession with social abstraction, is a commitment to a dualistic view of life, in effect separating mind from body. Capitalist consumerism has reduced life to a class structure of theatrical roles.

In the final two stories, the motives for exploitation return to those of part one (sexual indulgence) and each involves a misuse of imaginative vision. Don Gionni promises his friend, Pietro, that he can transform Pietro's wife, Gemmata, into a horse and back again into a woman. This promise of visual magic proves to be a trick on Don Gionni's part to lure Gemmata into sexual intercourse. His success is impeded by Pietro's vociferous protestations. "By speaking you have ruined it," says Don Gionni, but of course this is a rationalization. As in part one, language is already being destroyed by its use in exploiting others (the father of Caterina, Isabetta's brother, and Don Gionni all use words to lie); its decay is again reflected in the progressive ugliness of mouths (both Don Gionni and Pietro, as well as Isabetta's brother, are in need of dental work). More explicitly than in part one, images and the powers of vision are also decaying (voyeurism as a tool of exploitation, imagination as a ruse for adultery), and thus Don Gionni's episode ends with a shot of Gemmata turning away from the camera toward a wall, explicitly avoiding eye contact with the camera.

With the story of Tingoccio and Meuccio, visual illumination becomes overtly a factotum of sexual drive. Tingoccio dies from an overindulgence in sexual intercourse. He returns in a vision to his friend Meuccio and tells him that sex is counted as no sin in the afterlife. Meuccio then runs to a woman, who was formerly associated with Tingoccio, and jumps into bed with her. The very nature of his suppression and release is predicated on a fracture between physical and spiritual reality. The three elements of the trinary scheme—body, mind, and imagination—have moved toward a state of ever greater disjunction from their mildly positive potential in the Caterina episode and the preceding one which introduced the painter.

Giotto's progress also concludes in a dualism of sorts like that which flourishes in the stories which his presence frames. He is seen on several occasions observing people on the street as subjects for the fresco he has been commissioned to paint on the wall of the church. His method of viewing his subjects, framing them between his fingers, makes explicit the process of visual confinement occurring in the narrative. Moreover, the images sought by the painter will ultimately be placed within the frame of the painting. The ultimate frame is the church, institutionalized religion which, in conjunction with the middle-class urge for refinement, frames spiritual vision, particularly as embodied in the artistic powers of the painter. The result of this process tends to be a separation of art and life, and concurrently, the divorce of spirit and flesh, for the figures in the painter's fresco are not lifelike humans but idealized forms whose vertical ascendancy upon a wall marks their distance from their unrefined, physical origins. The exploitation of vision, as in the intervening narratives, breeds a disjunction of powers. The painter's fresco remains unfinished and the painter confesses his impotence to complete the work. His phrase, "Why produce a work of art when it's so nice just to dream about it," betrays his latent (and society's collective) desire to remove creative instincts from the concrete world out of which they are generated: they should dwell in an ideal static limbo. Mind, body, imagination are as divorced in the painter's story as they are in the stories he frames. Concluding the process of negation, he ends the film and his episode by turning, like Gemmata, away from the camera and from eye contact with external reality.

There is, of course, irony in the negative use of framing, for, cinematically, the frame is unavoidable. Pasolini's implication at this point in the trilogy seems to be that a film art which takes the frame itself as its primal substance rather than the vitality of the human form is bound finally to negate itself by virtue of the static nature of its conception. Life, the true subject of Pasolini's films, is inclined through natural pressures to break frames. However, in the concluding film of the trilogy, *The Arabian Nights*, "being in the frame" will indicate the immersion of art in life.

By and large, Pasolini's *Decameron* concerns itself with the misuse of the flesh, envisioning physical and sexual obsession as forces which destroy intelligence and imagination, leaving man's spiritual and physical lives disjointed. By their fear of physical reality (an obsession with flesh in reverse), religious institutions, or artistic powers working within them, fail to complete a synthesis of human experience, and seek shelter in dreams divorced from the world rather than an enrichment of experience within it. The final vision experienced by Pasolini as the painter is a dream along the lines of Giotto's *Last Judgment* in which those of spiritual inclination are separated from those of physical orientation. It is a dream of radical division: moreover, it encapsulates the major problems identified in the film: as a young couple in their nakedness are pushed down a hillside, the camera cuts to four nuns hiding their eyes. The camera then moves to a group of disconsolate men and a model of a church apparently held by one child. All the eyes are downcast and unseeing. The painter's imagination, the power of greatest synthesizing potential in the film, is left with a dream of disjunction and sorrow.

We may also note that natural love has been allowed to flower only once in the film, with Caterina and Riccardo. But they were the unlucky recipients of a trick of fate, being born into the same social class. The antiworld posture of institutional religion generates a confusion of love with lust or spiritual purity. If not this, love is smothered by the expanding middle-class aspirations for wealth.

Finally, while females dominate males in part one, the men return as the exploiters in part two. The stereotyping of social roles contingent upon the elaboration of bourgeois mentality separates and freezes the roles of men and women in a male-dominated society. In his succeeding films, Pasolini reveals this male ascendancy to be the foundation of Fascist consciousness, a neurotic compulsion to control and regulate, eliminating femininity entirely from the terrain of its soul. If feminine ascendancy results in directionless carnality, male dominance leads to the overvaluation of totally abstruse distinctions between men, such as class and business profit.

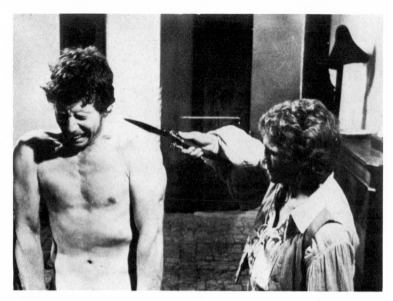

Evil triumphs in The Canterbury Tales: *(top) villains threaten dismemberment*
The Museum of Modern Art/Film Stills Archive

(bottom) the Devil atop the hill at the end of the film

11

The Canterbury Tales: Pilgrim's Egress

THE CANTERBURY TALES is the second film in Pasolini's "Trilogy of Life."[1] While it can be viewed as an autonomous work, it does carry forth the concerns of carnality and the artist's role in life established in *The Decameron*. While the first work concerns the vitiation of artistic power resulting from its confinement within an idealizing religious structure, *The Canterbury Tales* places the artist in a largely secular environment. In essence, the problem of the artist's relationship to life is moved from a confrontation with the Church to a confrontation with bourgeois materialism. The role of Chaucer (played by Pasolini) is an ambiguous one. On the one hand, he can be seen as the moral eye of the film, but, on the other hand, he seems to become a victim of the bourgeois concerns of his subjects, the pilgrims, who use art for diversion or self-congratulation. Like Giotto in *The Decameron*, he becomes more separated from the narrative, more isolated, and immobile. Perhaps because of this process, Pasolini has explicitly described Chaucer as "a bourgeois": "Chaucer still has one foot in the Middle Ages, but he is not 'of the people,' even though he took his stories from the people. He is already a bourgeois. He looks forward to the Protestant Revolution . . . with Chaucer there is already a kind of unhappy feeling, an unhappy conscience."[2] Perhaps Pasolini saw in Chaucer the makings of an overly judgmental artist with a tendency to withdraw from life—surely criticisms which one might level at Pasolini himself. And, again, *perhaps* this explains why Pasolini chose to play the role himself, in line with his liking for characters to be played by actors who in some way embody the nature to be portrayed. "I too," writes Pasolini, "am a bourgeois, in fact a petit bourgeois, a turd convinced that my stench is not only scented perfume, but is in fact the only perfume of the world."[3]

Moreover, in line with the trinary construction of the trilogy, while the evils of *The Decameron* "generally" center on sex and physical own-

143

ership, those in *The Canterbury Tales* tend to issue from more abstract concerns: profit, revenge, and an overzealous emphasis on control. Many episodes in the two films seem interchangeable, and surely there is a concern with abstraction revealed in the work of the painter in *The Decameron*. What one can say is that there is an "historical" difference in the films, the first being more medieval, more precapitalist (although the roots of capitalism are surely visible), and more concerned with conflicts in the arena of religion and profligacy, spirit and flesh; the second being more explicitly capitalist, centering on people who use the body less for pleasure than for monetary gain.

The Narrative Progress of *The Canterbury Tales*

The initial sequence of *The Canterbury Tales* invokes a reflection of the trinary model of life (body/mind/imagination) discussed in the previous chapter. The initial shot reveals the head of a man, eyes closed, sheltered in a whitish corner, singing of death. The camera swings to the right, leaving the singer out of the frame, to discover the face of a cowled man staring intently at the singer. With another move to the right, the camera leaves both weathered faces to focus on a pair of blond wrestlers, one of whom masters the other.

The eyes of the cowled man, our representation of vision, are fixated by the abstract words of the song. (This same sense of verbal dominance is present in the credit sequence, where the stark black and white titles which fill the screen seem to obfuscate the visible origins of the voices and noises on the soundtrack.) Neither singer nor watcher shows much interest in the delegates of physical power, the wrestlers.

The "fall" which the stronger wrestler wins resonates as a pun throughout the film (an appropriately witty joke for a film dealing with intellectuality). In its largest punning sense, *The Canterbury Tales* of Pasolini traces a *fall* from "tale" telling to "tail" telling—from the story-in-song of the opening frame to the vision of the devil's tail near film's end. This exotic "end" forms a metaphor of sorts of the excretory nature of existence which results from the obsession with profit and ownership. This passion for acquisition is portrayed in the film as an intellectual disease, a substitution of abstractions for concrete realities. We can see this process occurring not only within each of the tales, but in the activity of the camera as "tail" seer. By its obsession with fundaments and falling, it turns from the process of creation to that of elimination, most graphically, anal elimination.

The potential pun on falling entailed in the wrestlers' activity is taken up by the film in the initial movements of the camera—dropping from the trinary scheme to pilgrims and geese on the ground—and in the first shot of January (the protagonist of the first story) which reveals him entering the frame by descending a stairway. The camera follows this descent by panning downward, performing a visual enactment of "the fall." The element of the controlling intellect is also present here in the manner in which January proceeds to enthrone himself among his guests, talking incessantly, and imposing his will peremptorily upon them. Furthermore, we witness an initial "analization" of vision in the manner by which January chooses his bride: a child lifts the skirt of the stooped May, revealing her buttocks to January.

Pasolini's choice of "The Merchant's Tale" as the first story in his film implicates bourgeois capitalism as a force in the fall of man. Appropriately, this tale, perhaps more than any other in Chaucer's work, bears strong allusions to the myth of the Fall. Thus it contains an idyllic garden, a tree as the locus of a sin, an illumination of good and evil, and a banishment of sorts in the precipitant retreat of Demian. Pasolini's version contains all these elements plus a few more. The carefully trimmed garden with its phallic shrubs reveals not only the imposition of a rational and artificial will on nature but the operation of a rather blatant "anal complex"; in fact, the merging of the anal associations with the sense of control suggests a connection being drawn by Pasolini between "analization" and the dissociative nature of the dominantly abstract (and capitalist) approach to life: they are both attempts at retention rather than growth.

The events in January's garden also reincarnate the trinary system of the opening frames, for in May, January, and Demian we once again have examples of the powers of physicality (May and her characteristic arse), verbality (the visually alert Demian, who is attracted to May by her eyes rather than her bottom, and who exploits the superior power of his eyes to seduce May and escape the literally blind January). The return of sight to the old man paradoxically brings with it the expulsion of visual man—weak as he is—from both the garden and the film. With him goes the potential for unifying man's trinary dimensions. With a quick wit serving his mercantile possessiveness, January allows the reality of what he has seen (May with Demian) to be subdued by the verbal rationalizations of May. In essence, the word vanquishes the eye and we have a repetition of the story portrayed in the opening sequence— the ascendancy of words over visions, a dissociation of elements (not only are May and Demian not allowed to consummate their sexual activity but the three characters are never seen in the same frame) and an elimination (the vanquishing of the wrestler is repeated in Demian's banishment from the garden). Pasolini does not allow the Greek figures in the garden to be identified with specific names. They are, of course, in Chaucer's tale, Pluto and Persephone, human embodiments of the forces of death and regeneration, who, as such, imbue Chaucer's story with a symbolism deliberately lacking in Pasolini's version. In the latter's story, age triumphs over youth, ownership (associated with the capitalist predilection of the Merchant) squelches freedom.

While the choice of "The Merchant's Tale" as the lead story establishes the theme of bourgeois decadence in life, the problem of the bourgeois approach to art has already been intimated in Pasolini's use of the innkeeper, himself a bourgeois merchant of sorts, to initiate the idea of storytelling on the pilgrimage. His motive, a desire to "beguile the time," is innocent enough except for the fact that it exploits art for his own "commercial" interest and represents an attitude Pasolini has consistently disparaged in such works as *Accatone* and *Mamma Roma*. Art used as a cosmetic diversion is precisely what Pasolini hates about the bourgeoisie.

The presentation of sexual activity in the film reveals clearly the destructive operation of the bourgeois mentality in conjunction with the desire for profit and verbal control. Pasolini depicts a linkage between exploitation (a bourgeois trademark) and abstraction. Despite all of their limitations, January, May, and Demian evince a visible interest in, and realization of, life potential in the images around them. They seem to take a joy in sex for its own sake, and sex, in turn, is shown in a relatively positive light within their story. January, with the onset of blindness, even seems about to transcend his limited sexual interest in May for an emotional involvement as well. His pathetic cry for his "wife" invokes a degree of emotional as well as commercial concern.

But, in the stories following this tale, we witness a continual decline in the joy of sexual activity, due not to its "inherent" evil but to the exploitative, abstract interests of profit and ownership which impinge upon it. Hence, in the episode which follows January's ("The Summoner's Tale"), we are shown sexual activity deliberately repressed for commercial gain and even punished. The Summoner operates by spying on homosexual activities and blackmailing the participants. Thus, in his figure, both the eyes and the body are reduced to "markets" for monetary profit, tools of the pocketbook. He is a proto-capitalist, filling the moneybag by exploiting the body. All of this entails a restriction in life vision which is translated into cinematic language by Pasolini. The shots are made through narrow openings, limiting our perception of the events. This contraction of vision forces the viewer into the role of voyeur, perceiving events from the position of the Devil, who is spying on the Summoner through cracks in doors, just as the Summoner is spying upon his prey. And, since that prey is engaged in anal sex, we have a sort of analization of our own vision—a peering into the "tail"—which foreshadows the conclusion of the film. Although sex is again being enjoyed for its own sake, the transition from heterosexual to homosexual activity presages the increasing segregation of men and women in the film (e.g., Chaucer and his wife).

In "The Cook's Tale," which follows, commercial exploitation is associated with prostitution for the first time. Moreover, as the prostitute offered the Chaplinesque protagonist (Ninetto Davoli) by his companion is also the latter's wife, capitalism is shown splitting apart the sacred union, marriage, its sexual dimensions being a convenient business. Before the deal is consummated, the police arrest the participants and lock the protagonist in a pillory. His confinement is the natural outcome of his own practice of a kind of prostitution: the debasement of his magical, imaginative powers. His gift for life is evoked for us by his likeness, in dress and gesture, to the most magical of screen figures, Charlie Chaplin, and also by his manifestation of supernatural powers: for example, he can drop a basket of eggs without cracking a shell, then magically transfer the eggs back to the basket. His "fall" from artist to capitalist occurs shortly afterward when he deigns to participate in a dice game, a parody of capitalist economics by which profit is derived through the exploitation of the gamblers. The real magical powers of the Chaplinesque figure are jettisoned for a game of monetary profit based on endowing abstract numbers with value. When the hero spills the eggs a second time (after being discovered gambling by his master), they simply break. Spiritual power has been sold for material power, creativity for mere abstract gaming, the artistic for the bourgeois. While Chaplin, in his films, usually discovers freedom through the exercise of a humanist imagination (*The Gold Rush, Easy Street, City Lights*), his parody, having prostituted imagination, is conversely imprisoned. His activity defines for us a model of the fate of the artist in a world impelled by profit.

The end of the Cook's sequence provides another significant comment on the fall of the artist, for the head of the protagonist juts from the pillory, visually dissociated from the rest of his body. His debasement of his spiritual energy fosters the fragmentation of the natural mind-body tension, the two splitting apart as in *The Decameron*. This trend waxes dominant in the rest of the film. The dissociative overtones of the film's opening scene are reevoked as the pilloried Ninetto sings the song first sung by the man in the initial frame. The imaginative powers he evinced on occasion (as in his imagining the members of a wedding party naked and dancing) have been reduced to the verbal. Perhaps here more than in any other single episode we see the bourgeois mind delineated in terms of commercialism, greed, the prostitution of self-inhering powers, and, in the meta-cinematic arena, the subordination of the visual to the verbal.

"The Miller's Tale" carries the corruption of the sexual act to a parody of the homoeroticism of "The Summoner's Tale," for Nicholas "ends up" with a red-hot prong from the blacksmith's shop inserted in his fundament. Yet as we move to the next story, a restoration of sexual value seems to be at hand as Pasolini cuts directly from the howling Nicholas to the Wife of Bath having sex with her husband on the same bed used by Nicholas and Allison in the previous tale. The illusion is soon destroyed when we learn that the wife's husband is dying from too much sexual exertion. Thus, coitus is now directly associated with death and, as each husband's death increases the widow's inherited wealth, with the acquisition of material goods. The Wife is another proto-capitalist, who makes marriage a profitable business. Her activity entails new exaggerations in the separation of mind and body. Hence, with her husband's death, Pasolini cuts to the Wife's seduction of an Oxford student. While she desperately flogs his sexual organs in an attempt to arouse him, he buries his face obliviously in a book. Intellectual and sexual instincts are totally sundered. Appropriately, their marriage is allowed to conclude with only a parody of sexual intercourse: the Wife viciously biting the student's nose, oral acts here replacing genital sex. The final image of the tale parallels that of "The Cook's Tale," presenting two heads totally dissociated from bodily functions, visually and thematically.

In the tale of the two students which follows, sex is unequivocally reduced to a means of vengeance for commercial exploitation. Two students are swindled by a miller and decide to take their revenge on his wife and daughter. Hence, the students are not primarily interested in the women at the mills, but in the flour out of which they have been cheated, itself a small portion. They seduce the miller's wife and daughter, then, as a means of "getting even."

The increasing ugliness of the intrusion of bourgeois rationality into the realm of love is marked by the increasing ugliness of the people involved. The women are hardly the goddesses of January's garden or even those of the Cook's dream; the students themselves are dirty, pimply adolescents, a far cry from the handsome Demian who attracted May. They are only slightly more repellent than the Wife of Bath and her student, who in turn were debased replacements for Nicholas and Allison. The human visage, like the mouths in *The Decameron*, is a signpost of decaying spiritual potential.

We move from the two students to the tale of four brothers (who are, again, even uglier than their precursors), in which sexual activity is completely dissociative (oral sex, as presented here, radically separates the persons involved and the use of the whip further eliminates sex from sexual activity). The penis, in short, is reduced from its potential in the tale of January as a life-giver to being merely a tool of bodily elimination. Thus, the central act of the first part of the story is urination on an audience. Moreover, the tale shows us explicitly the process of elimination inherent in the bourgeois, money-oriented mind: the brothers kill each other off for sole possession of a pile of gold coins (significantly inscribed with images of the human head). Activity in the film has become increasingly controlled by the head, implying not that the protagonists are intellectuals, but that their interest in acquisition is an interest in abstraction, and that their greed is, itself, cinematically an evolved result of the verbally dominant, visually dead man pictured in frame one. Appropriately, the brothers are themselves reduced to abstract silhouettes, dying painfully from nausea and diarrhea.

From here there is only one place left to go—hell, which is exactly where we are taken. Overt sex is now wholly eliminated from human activity, or reduced to a hand probing the extremities of a dying man: one merchant "feels" another on his deathbed, looking for hidden money. Emphasizing the growing sense of psychic contraction, "The Friar's Tale" opens with a shot of a merchant neatly framed in a window. Bourgeois aggrandizement at its worst is the primary subject, with the merchant attempting to bilk a dying man of his money by opening a chest out of the sight of the victim. Appropriately, the bourgeois gentleman is finally commanded to close his eyes by an angel, the manifest destiny toward which the film has driven, and allow himself to be led by the angel child to hell. The process of dissociation entails the elimination of the eyes, and finally, in hell, the camera focuses on the Devil's anus as it expels miniature devils. The powers of creation—tale-telling—have thus reduced themselves punningly to powers of excretion and exhaustion—tail-telling. No wonder the film closes on the smirking visage of Pasolini himself.

Marriage

The degenerative trend regarding sexual activity and profit is most obviously paralleled by the increasingly disruptive quality of marriage within the film. Thus while January and May are in some sense reconciled, the following marriages are marked by increasing perversion and dissociation. For the Summoner, marriage is union with the Devil; for the apprentice in "The Cook's Tale," it becomes a means of prostitution; for the Wife of Bath, it is a commercial game; for Nicholas in "The Miller's Tale," an obstacle to be hurdled; and for the miller and his wife, a commercial union for deceiving customers. The most profound marriage being disrupted is that between the three dimensions of man envisioned in the trinary model of the opening frames (vision, intellect, and physicality). In fact, with the reduction of vision or visual man, man increasingly becomes a binary rather than trinary possibility in which mind and body begin to separate, as with the image of the Oxford student lost in his book while his genitals are stimulated. This particular trend shows up pronouncedly in the images of Chaucer himself as he appears in the narrative, for his story is one of continual decline and isolation.

Chaucer is initially shown moving on foot, confronting a man of images, the bizarrely tatooed figure at the inn. We next see him immobilized in his study, writing with pen, apparently assuming the role of monolithic narrative voice for the tales (Pasolini has dropped any sense of relationship between tales and tellers); but, despite his creative endeavor, he is also dissociating himself from people, the material of his work. (There is, of course, no absolute visual evidence in the film that he has any creative relationship to the narrative at all.) Hence, he fulminates at one man with a cat and suffers the wrath of his wife in the next scene, his own marriage becoming part of the general marital malaise.

His final appearance restates the mind/body dissociation so prevalent in the other stories. Following the shot of the Devil's hind quarters, there is a cut to Chaucer smiling. Three significant details appear in this scene. First, the color potential has been reduced to black and white—he wears a white gown and is posed against a pure black background—suggesting both a reduction of his life potential and his incarceration in a binary world. Second, the two shots of him dissociate head and hand, synecdoches generally in Pasolini's works of mind and body, concept and act.

Thus we first see his face, then a shot of his isolated hand writing the conclusion. Finally, we see the abstractions of language, the logical end of the verbally abstractive beginning, urging one to look away from the work by reference to the "higher" powers ("Amen"). Pasolini's *Canterbury Tales* forms a bizarre epic of the dissociative end of the middle-class attempt to locate value in abstractions stripped of people (wealth, God, vengeance, romantic ideals): to separate meaning from experience, especially visual experience.

The destruction of light is another related motif of the general "fall." It is carried out in the film most obviously in the verbal conclusion and in the angel's injunction to the bourgeois gentleman to close his eyes. But we can see the same tendency in the deployment of color. If the early scenes are rich in colors and possibilities, the latter scenes are progressively poorer in them. Essentially less and less variety is allowed on the screen until the final, lifeless black and white is all that remains. But even in the early color patterns we can see the inherent dissociation, for the colors neatly divide the humans who bear them. Thus we see people in robes which are stark violet on one side and solid green on the other, or red and yellow in the same fashion. All of the additive and subtractive primaries are present, yet flagrantly dissociated, visually suggesting the dissociation of the people who wear them. From this point, varieties diminish until we arrive at a basically grey, colorless hell in which devils are either green or red. Color possibility has been reduced to a conflict of opposites and this is further reduced to basic black and white. The story of color in the film, therefore, repeats the process of elimination carried out on the human level which results in the excreting anus at film's end. The life of exploitation and dissociation of oneself from the currents of life is the elimination of life.

If his *Decameron* presents a degeneration of intellect through bodily indulgence, Pasolini's *Canterbury Tales* is the other side of the coin, a portrait of bourgeois values which have forgotten physical, sexual realities.

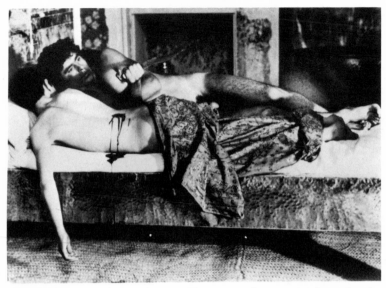

Phallic violence in Arabian Nights: *(top) Shazaman in sleep unwittingly murders the prince, (bottom) sexual contact becomes symbolic—Aziz (Ninetto Davali) threatens Budur*
The Museum of Modern Art/Film Stills Archive

12

The Arabian Nights: The Flowering of Feminine Spirit

AS THE CONCLUDING FILM in the "Trilogy of Life," *The Arabian Nights* (*The Flower of the 1001 Nights* in the Italian version) consummates the issues of the two preceding films, finally bestowing upon the trilogy a vision of life more optimistic than that of its bleak and somber precursors. *The Arabian Nights* is one of Pasolini's few positive works, a condition it aspires to by portraying the creative possibilities of humanity more than its unappealing probabilities. Still, as a positive film, its celebration of life has definite limits. The victory of love and self-liberation central to the story is more one of "accommodation" than total spiritual release. The established powers of the world, responsible for fostering and sustaining a capitalist mentality based on sexual exploitation, are vanquished not in fact but through temporarily fooling them, exploiting the ensconced errors of the system against it. Thus a young slave girl, Zumurrud in the disguise of a man, becomes the king of a city through the uncritical worship of maleness by its inhabitants.

Let us first consider the manner by which *The Arabian Nights* fulfills the "Trilogy of Life." This complementarity has a number of threads to it. As in the earlier works, *The Arabian Nights* concerns itself a great deal with art and artists. While the earlier films present artists sequestered, willingly, from life, whose works tend to become idealized and divorced from their actual subject matter, *The Arabian Nights* places the artist and the artistic imagination in the arena of human action, choice, and self-determination. Zumurrud, as we shall see, is both an artisan (a weaver) and the architect of her life and her lover's. By extension, in the meta-cinematic realm of the work, the dimension by which art takes art as its subject matter (the "ontology of narrative,"[1] in Pasolini's phrase), *The Arabian Nights* tells the story of the imagination, its liberation of new form, and, specifically, the moral nature of narrative as both an educator and an awakener of consciousness. It is through his

153

exposure to art, particularly narrative, that Nur ed Din is made worthy
of Zumurrud.

By its emphasis upon imagination and creativity as benevolent powers, *The Arabian Nights* fulfills the latent trinary structure implicit in
Pasolini's trilogy (as discussed in the preceding chapters). If *The Decameron*, by comparison, deals extensively with things physical (the
exploitation of the body) and *The Canterbury Tales* with the abstraction
of profit, *The Arabian Nights* portrays, despite its darker corners, life
sustained by and breaking out through the internal pressure of an
organic imagination: life becomes creative process. The emphasis upon
"flower" in the Italian title is doubly significant, for events often "blos-
som" in this film by a magical logic which transcends cause and effect.
The movie is a narrative of the unexpected and coincidental, "destiny"[2]
in Pasolini's phrase, but destiny understood less as determinism than as
the continual revelation of creative possibility latent in the nature of life
and conditions of existence. Indeed, "being" in an apt cinematic sense
(celebrating motion) is manifested as "becoming" in this film, Pasolini's
existential personality dominating his Marxist-Freudian side. It is those
who resist the invitation to grow through art and love (both quietly present in the universe of the film) who are doomed; indeed, they are
crucified.

But, of course, *The Arabian Nights* is not without its political edges.
While comprising a rather radical feminist statement—women are the
vessels and generators of all the powers of love, intellect, and creativity[3]—the film also extends the general study of capitalist evolution,
which runs through the "Trilogy of Life," to a phase in which it is transcended in a surprising manner. While the society of *The Decameron*
is largely nascently bourgeois (suffering primarily from the inability to
experience a holistic integration of spirit and flesh), and that of *The Canterbury Tales* explicitly late bourgeois (profit and money being the dominant destroyers of life), the society of *The Arabian Nights*, although
historically prebourgeois, is a little of both and yet, by its particular communal vision, almost postcapitalist. In an important sense, what is
achieved and pictured for us at the end of the film is a largely communal
world in which male dominance (always associated with exploitation in
Pasolini films, from *Accatone* onward) has been superseded by a feminine order, which in fact contains both sexes, both principles. "Integration," then, is a crucial and pervasive act in this movie. Spirit and flesh,
mind and body, art and life—the types of dualistic splits which normally concern Pasolini—are transcended, or, more accurately, are not

given the opportunity to ramify. The essential Pasolini condition, that our experience is holistic by nature and splintered through misperception, finds its most complete expression in this film.

The Narrative Progress of *The Arabian Nights*

Both the Marxist and existentialist dimensions of the movie are presented rather straightforwardly in the opening scene. In the narrow confines of an alleylike market area in Bagdad we see a slave girl, Zumurrud, led to a selling block on which she will be auctioned off. There is a sense of confinement created by the narrow street and, conversely, a sense of freedom and possibility bestowed upon the scene by the flow of life through the corridor; the colorfulness of the people and a general air of mystery and beauty, a result of the careful lighting and photography which emphasizes the colors of gold and amber, mitigating the somberness of the occasion. Nevertheless, the situation conveys a literal Marxist view of capitalist society: a world in which the human being is brutally reduced to a commercial product, an object for a privileged consumer society. The existentialist shade to the situation is present in the fact that Zumurrud, though being sold, will be granted a marginal degree of self-determination in her future: she will be allowed to choose her new master. Out of this small chink in the armor of the male-dominated community, from a slender thread of free choice, Zumurrud fashions a complete liberation from her imposed indentureship, using her imagination and intelligence.

This actualization of freedom is, of course, contingent upon Zumurrud's perspicacity, her ability to see into the heart of things at a glance. Thus she disqualifies one applicant for the inability of his "cane" to sustain an erection and chooses instead the unlikely person of Nur ed Din, an innocent and smooth-faced youth, who proves to be capable of love, though a bit thick-witted. Throughout this episode, Zumurrud is presented as a free spirit, a joyous girl who takes pleasure in the perturbation she excites in her male chauvinist audience by her affront to their overwhelming obsession with masculinity. Her first misadventure (being stolen from Nur ed Din) results from an act of revenge on the part of an outraged bidder offended at the slighting of his virility.

But Zumurrud's misfortune is less a product of her own aggression than of Nur ed Din's stupidity. He has much to learn! Sent to the market to sell a rug (woven by Zumurrud) with explicit instructions not to sell to anyone with blue eyes, Nur ed Din quickly falls prey to the blue-eyed Christian, Berhoun, who, by arousing his male ego, inveigles Nur ed Din into eating drugged food and steals Zumurrud. Miraculously, through a female grapevine, Zumurrud arranges an escape; but, characteristic of woeful male perception throughout the movie, Nur ed Din falls asleep at the critical moment, allowing Zumurrud to climb down a wall into the hands of another thief who has stumbled upon the scene by chance. She is chained to a stake with a male guard, but does not lose her wits. Lulling the guard to sleep with her charms, she chains him up, steals his clothes, and enters the world newly born as a male. Or, at least, she might as well be, for the males she encounters fail to perceive her disguise.

She arrives at the city of Sair, whose population, still mourning the recent death of their king, is awaiting the arrival of the first male to their city who, according to custom, must be offered the crown. Thus through the conjunction of male imperception and destiny in the role of chance, Zumurrud manages to transform herself from slave to king, manipulating the male domination of the world through her self-created role, or image.

In a large thematic sense, the energies of femininity have won their release from indentureship to male hegemony; the next major task along these lines of sexual politics will be the liberation of the male from his own prison. Thematically, this liberation, centered primarily on Nur ed Din, involves a somewhat more complicated series of steps. The first phase in this process involves the destruction of maleness in its most fascistic, pernicious form. Thus the two thieves who abducted Zumurrud arrive in Sair in quest of her only to be brought before the new king. While Zumurrud recognizes each one immediately, they, woefully imperceptive, dead in the eyes, fail to recognize her. They are fortuitously dispatched by crucifixion.

Nur ed Din's education has begun somewhat before this, however, with the aid of Zumurrud. Through her, he is initiated into the joint realms of sex and art as she takes him to bed and then reads him one of the stories from *The Thousand and One Nights*. The episode she chooses to read is one of the fragments involving Harun Al Rashid, his wife, Zeudi, and his poet, Sium. Harun espies a young girl bathing in a pool and returns to his caravan to ask Sium if the poet can compose some verses equal to his vision. Sium, who has spied Harun spying on the girl, composes a bantering verse which encapsulates all of this. Everyone laughs; Sium returns to his tent, picking up three young men on the way, and all retire to a night of feasting, sexual activity (though not explicit), and poetry reading. Meanwhile, Harun and Zeudi have each picked up a young companion of the same sex. Berhame, the youth found by Harun, tells the latter that he intends not to marry because of the perfidious nature of women. His reluctance proves weak when Harun and Zeudi, in a contest to see which of the two adolescents is more attractive, arrange to have the two drugged and placed, naked, side by side. They are awakened at different times and, in turn, seduce each other, each having fallen prey to the other's charms.

The story, being at odds with the characteristics of the world inhabited by Zumurrud, provides an ideal model of relationship between the sexes. Harun and Zeudi conclude that Berhame and Giana are of equal beauty and power, that one sex is not superior to the other: "The one is the mirror to the other." The story also provides an oblique reference to Nur ed Din via the education of Berhame. The latter boy clearly suffers a change of heart regarding women—"God's will be done," he says—an education, so to speak, which is also the process in which Nur ed Din is engaged. Destiny or God's will, as it is referred to, must be done. For the most part, that destiny involves learning to love. Those who learn receive the fruits of "destiny" largely as a reward. Nur ed Din's love, being flawed by youthful egoism, needs tempering.

Also implicit in this episode, by Sium's activity, is a model of the relationship between life and art. Raw experience becomes aesthetic experience, either in its own right or in the form of poetry, and that experience is directed back into life as a power which intensifies and awakens one to the possibilities of fulfillment. Thus Harun's voyeurism becomes a poem, and the poem becomes an occasion for delight, generating further contacts, further poetry. This same process pervades the short episode of Sium's feast with the boys, for they "arouse" and are aroused by poetry. In the case of Barsum and Giana, the drugged youths, their response to the aesthetic power of each other draws them into conjunction. Figures converge under the sign of a poetic spirit which renders them selfless yet intensely alive.

It is this same service of aesthetic education which the other narratives, told to Nur ed Din at the Casa of Munis, provide him. Nur ed Din, in quest of the stolen Zumurrud, is captured by three girls, "Munis," "Budur," and "Nahbuda." On the roof of her house, Munis proposes to read from *The Thousand and One Nights*. The story she chooses, that of Taji al Moluk, is really a tale-within-a-tale which Pasolini has expanded with the annexation of two other highly modified stories from other parts of the collection. The episode regarding Taji frames the other three tales; that is, they are told to Taji as tools to modify his awareness

of life just as they in some sense are meant to do for Nur ed Din. Thus
the conjunctive relationship of art, life, and love is maintained.

Appropriately, each of the tales which Taji (and Nur ed Din, the
audience) hears involves a model of male egoism. Taji, however, eludes
the snares of male arrogance as he benefits from his education and learns
to court and win the Princess Dunya through aesthetic means. She, on
the other hand, has vowed to turn from life to practice asceticism.
Dunya's monastic sensibility has resulted from a bad dream in which
a male dove abandons his mate in a hunter's net after being freed himself by his mate. Dunya concludes that marriage is therefore useless,
that all males are evil. Taji wins her over through art: he constructs a
mosaic in a cupola in the garden which depicts the male dove liberating its mate and the two flying off together. Dunya is eventually rein-
tegrated with life, a victory for holism and imagination.

Three Interpolated Tales

En route to this union, Taji hears three tales of male failure. The first,
told to him by Aziz, deals with the failure of Aziz to distinguish real love
from false, to perceive the needs and sufferings of others. Betrothed to
his cousin, Aziza, Aziz, on his wedding day, remembers a friend he has
neglected to invite to the ceremony. On his way to rectify the error, he
sees a mysterious girl in a window who speaks to him in a strange sign
language. Enamored of her, he forgets to return to his wedding. Aziza,
when she hears the story, selflessly translates the signs for Aziz and generally aids him in his pursuit of the mystery woman. Aziz blithely gads
along his course unaware of the heartbreak all of this has caused Aziza.
Wrapped in his own little world, he is largely unaware of things outside
him. Like Nur ed Din, he tends to fall asleep at inappropriate times,
demonstrating a weakness in concern for his would-be lover. Thus the
tale provides an appropriate lesson for Nur ed Din, whose thick-witted
dozing has resulted twice in Zumurrud's abduction. Aziza eventually
pines away from neglect, and Budur, the mystery woman (who, we are
to believe, has been unaware of the aid Aziza has rendered Aziz) orders
Aziz to do penance for a year. Instead, he marries a rich girl, then
returns to Budur a year later expecting to be greeted with open arms.
For his blundering unconsciousness and lack of feeling, Aziz is castrated
upon Budur's orders, an appropriate end for one who has perceived in
the opposite sex only an opportunity for self-gratification.

The second story, told by Shazaman, involves foolish bravado which endangers the girl he claims to love. Surviving an ambush of his cavern, Shazaman wanders to a city inhabited by bandits, where he is given shelter by one of the few honest denizens. While gathering firewood, he discovers a trap door in the ground and inside a young girl who is the prisoner of a demon genie (Franco Citti, of course) who ravishes her nightly. Shazaman and the girl fall in love and he vows to save her. Informed of a secret code on a shield through which the genie can be summoned, Shazaman, in a moment of bravado and arrogance, strikes the magic words, disclaiming fear of the demon. However, with the impending arrival of the genie, he sprints with the fervor of a true coward for his home and safety. He is, nevertheless, discovered by the genie, who slays the girl in front of his eyes. Demonstrating the power of female love, she never flinches. Shazaman is carried away by the demon and told to be transformed into what his true nature dictates. He becomes a monkey. He is saved from this eternal fate when a girl, recognizing his fate through Shazaman's undiminished ability to write words (like Aziz, he functions mainly through symbols), kisses him appropriately and restores him. She, however, is immediately consumed in flames, another model of self-sacrificing femininity. Shazaman, now humiliated and aware of his foolishness, becomes a mendicant. While his ascetic choice is not a particularly acceptable model of a relationship to life, it exists primarily as the reward for a life of arrogance in dealing with life forces greater than oneself. Individuation is not to be confused with the arrogant assertion of one's ego. Shazaman must cleanse himself before returning to life fully and this he does by practicing art, specifically, mosaic stonework. Art functions as an education and a direct means of personal salvation.

The final story of the group is that of a young prince, Yunan, and that of an even younger prince, Asceta, who is killed by Yunan. Yunan hears the disembodied voice of God command him to go to an island; he complies, but his boat is shipwrecked on a different island. The voice returns, telling him of a copper, mechanical man in a cupola atop the hill who must be pushed into the ocean to make the waters navigable. Yunan achieves the deed, swims out into the sea, and lands on an island where he witnesses a young boy being placed underground. When he learns that the boy fears for his life because of a prediction that he would die as a sacrifice for the copper knight, Yunan assures the youth he will protect him. Destiny triumphs, and Yunan, in a trance, kills the boy. The contours of this tale, as in Shazaman's, suggest the foolishness of the personal ego in the face of mysterious forces beyond it: a kind of allegory, though disturbing, of Pasolini's sense of the individual's need to be integrated with the indwelling spirit of the universe.

Given the particularly brutal context, one might complain that as a moral lesson it is a bit like taking a bath in dirty water. Of what value is a God and a destiny which totally control men, exact primitive sacrifices, and play games with absurd symbols? A destiny which seems to require total submission of the self-generative power of the individual—a stark contrast to what is literally shown through Zumurrud. In answer to this, one can reply that these internal tales are clearly meant to display male faults and perceptual problems rather than supply models of Pasolini's ideal universe. Yunan is fooled because he thinks he can buck an obviously stronger power of life.

From another angle, Yunan's story touches upon a meta-cinematic dimension of the film regarding sign language, language in general, and symbolic form. As noted in the tale of Shazaman and Aziz, codes, signs, and symbols play a large role, yet their operation is strongly antiverbal, perhaps antisemiotic. It is through his fascination with Budur's sign language that Aziz is drawn into his ill-fated romance. His story suggests, in fact, that it is the substitution of symbolic form for actual life which causes, or symptomizes, his failure. In a holistic universe, symbols are abstractions from the organic whole and must not be confused with reality itself. Aziz, however, consistently substitutes symbols for reality, first in the signs of Budur, second in his making her a symbol of love (and therefore neglecting Aziza), and finally in his sexual encounter with her which is *wholly symbolic* in the film—he penetrates her with a bronze phallus mounted on the tip of an arrow. No other form of sexual relationship is shown us in his story. In the metaprocess of the story, Aziza herself is finally killed as a result of her indulgence in this code game. Pasolini's injunctions against "symbolism" are legion; likewise are his criticisms of linguistic, "verbal" semiology as applied to film. He is surely evoking both notions in these stories.

Shazaman's relationship is more arrogant than Aziz's: he assaults the code on the shield with impunity. Of course, the fabricator of the code is a demon and Shazaman's transformation into his "true form," a scrivener monkey, suggests his reality is a function of words (i.e., he is a braggadocio). His transition to visual artist, like Yunan's, must be seen as an advancement.

Along the lines of meta-cinema, the Yunan episode is deeply devoted to the problem of meanings abstracted from life (the disembodied voice which controls Yunan) and to stationary symbolic forms which control people's lives (the mechanical man in his remote cupola). What literally occurs in the episode is the destruction of one by the other: "the word" bumps off the static symbol, through Yunan, then kills the young prince. As the voice of nature, it is none too pleasant. On the other hand, it is a male voice and thus fascistic in the context of the movie. Hence, while the destruction of the copper man entails a liberation from control by dead symbols, it also engenders a liberation from *masculine* form and symbol which, of course, is the core of the sexual polemic of the film. The position and condition of the copper figure manifest the sad nature of extreme male dominance: divorce from the world, fascistic control, destructiveness, and lifeless mechanicalness. The controlling male voice renders itself extinct, as Yunan extinguishes the prince. Maleness has become overtly self-destructive.

The Yunan episode is the fulcrum of the movie, for following its fable of the end of male control by static symbol, the currents of the movie flow toward sexual conjunction, marriage, and the sort of fulfillment characteristic of comedic form. Dunya, the ascetic recluse, upon seeing Taji's mosaic (built by Yunan and Shazaman), is won over to him, and Nur ed Din, outside both stories, leaves to find Zumurrud. One immediate question arises in regard to the mosaic: if Yunan's story proclaims the end of control by symbolic form, what is the function of the painting? To which one responds that the painting is neither abstract nor really symbolic, symbol being necessarily defined as a respresentation which becomes a substitute for reality. The painting is as much about itself as it is about Taji or Dunya. But barring all of this, they do not choose to substitute it for reality (in the manner Aziz is shown doing with his phallic arrow) but as a tool to reintegrate themselves with living rather than symbolic figures. Such communion, in the logic of the film, is the true function of art, neither to symbolize nor communicate abstract meaning, but to bring about communion by awakening consciousness to the full potential of experiences: to invigorate, not control.

The Main Narrative Resumes: Reunion and Resolution

The dialectical tension between living and symbolic form sustains itself through the remainder of the story, which features the reunion of Nur ed Din and Zumurrud. In the swimming pool episode following the reading of Yunan's story, the girls tease Nur ed Din by applying exotic names to their sexual organs. When he finally grasps the nature of the game, he responds in kind. Yet this gamesmanship is really only a sub-

stitute of symbols for sexual activity. The best it does is remind Nur ed
Din of Zumurrud and he takes his leave minutes later at the first opportunity. He has been aroused in some manner by the stories, for his activity is now characterized by awakening rather than sleeping (he leaves
while the girls sleep) and by humility rather than concern for his ego.
Thus on encountering a figure of destiny in the guise of a lion, he does
not challenge it in Yunan or Shazaman fashion, but throws himself at its
feet and begs for help or an end to his sorrows. The lion then leads him
to Zumurrud's city. As in most places in his story, destiny appears more
as reward than as control (as it does in Yunan's case). Nur ed Din is
saved by his thorough lack of pretension, his demonstration of love for
Zumurrud, and capacity to yield and receive from others.

   With the reunion of Zumurrud and Nur ed Din, we witness a final
casting off of symbolic form. To reveal herself to Nur ed Din, she
removes her kingly robes and the symbolic male headpiece she sports as
ruler of the city. This final revelation resolves ironically the issue of symbolic form: it suggests that symbols are useful, especially in a world that
worships them. Zumurrud's role of king involves, in its sexual disguise,
a blending of symbolic with natural form. In her most private moments,
she divests herself of the artificial.

The Frame

   The placing of stories within stories provides *The Arabian Nights*
with a sandwich construction by which one story creates a frame around
another, encapsulating it. Thus the adventures of Zumurrud and Nur
ed Din provide a frame around the other episodes, such as that of Taji,
which, in turn, frames the stories of Aziz, which partly frame the stories
of Shazaman and Yunan.

   Now just as *The Arabian Nights* transforms the material of *The
Decameron* (that is, it transforms similar stories into comedic rather than
tragic vision), so the use of framing is transformed from its function in
the earlier film. While the deliberate positioning of figures inside frames
in *The Decameron* forms a corollary to their self-limiting, rigid mode
of perception, or manner of rendering the world fixed and benign, the
same process in *The Arabian Nights*, in its context of creative joy and
the use of art in rendering life more whole, directly associates the very
notion of "being in the frame" with the value of "being in the movie."
And in the film's comedic context, "to be in the movie" is to be open to
the possibilities of awakening, love, and the experience of creation, to
accept the wholeness of life.

One of the models of this comedic function of the frame is the hitherto discussed mosaic of Shazaman. The mosaic is not *one* still picture but a *series* of framed images which, though not literally in motion, nevertheless create a narrative through images. The frames manifest action and change, in effect creating a miniature movie. By choosing to live out in actuality the story of these frames, Dunya releases herself from a sequestered life of frustration and implacable desires to join the movie as she joins life.

Similarly, as the film draws to a close, as Zumurrud approaches the moment in which she will reveal herself to Nur ed Din, we see her moving sequentially through a series of frames in her background: a large mirror, a painting of a Renaissance woman. In fact, the room is filled with picture frames. Zumurrud is wholly within the film, so to speak, wholly within the world of wonder and magic, and wholly within a narrative art in which narration and life become fused, in which the individual manifests both a self-integrity and a participation in a process larger than himself.

13

Salo: Death Deco

PASOLINI'S LAST FILM derives its title from the area of Salo in northern Italy, which served as the last stronghold for Mussolini during World War II. Il Duce, however, has been replaced by four Fascists whose occupations link them with the foundations of society: a magistrate, a bishop, a duke, and a banker. Moreover, their retreat is practiced not as a military maneuver but as a means of satisfying their most primitive and perverse desires. Pasolini has taken the basic idea of this retreat from the Marquis de Sade's *120 Days of Sodom*, structuring the material loosely on the circular form of Dante's *Inferno*, developing his own work as a layered descent into the center of sadism, where the impulse for power and control over others is allowed to run unchecked to its logical end.

The events of Pasolini's film begin in an area around Marzabota, where an entire village was exterminated by the Fascists, and move toward Salo,[1] where the four libertines incarcerate themselves and their prey in a villa which is decorated in the combined styles of Art Deco and Italian Bauhaus.

Pasolini conceived the film as an attack on "consumerism" and power politics: "My film is planned as a sexual metaphor, which symbolizes in a visionary way, the relationship between exploiter and exploited. In sadism and in power politics human beings become objects . . . yes and something more: I want to attack the permissiveness of our new ways. So far society has repressed us. Now it offers a false front of permissiveness. One of the characters in my film says, in fact; 'While society represses everything, man can do anything. When society begins to permit something, only that something can be done.' This is the terrible bottom of our new liberties. A greater conformism than before."[2] All of this sounds, frankly, a little Jesuitical and one-sided; whatever is included by Pasolini in the "new permissiveness," which he leaves conveniently

165

vague, few of us are ready to sacrifice democracy, freedom of speech, sexual liberation, or our own consumer convenience to return to a medieval aristocracy or a totalitarian Communist state.

Besides the dubious one-sided pessimism of Pasolini's views on the contemporary world embodied in Salo, there are a couple of more direct complaints which have been leveled at the film: (1) that it only shows us a condition without delineating the cause (Barthes)[3] and (2) that it paints an image of the world patently inaccurate, i.e., we are not all sadistic Fascists nor submissives to fascism (New York reviewers).

In regard to the first objection, it may be argued that within the film causes are implicit in effects, power for power's sake; moreover, the film is not merely a catalog of tortures but an exploration of problems which have concerned Pasolini throughout his career: dualism, conformism, the nature of obsessive consumerism, and the relationship of man and nature. The film presents a vision of complex, predatory, consumer fulfillment, a condition which Pasolini seems to have felt, at the time of the film's creation, to be surfacing again in the world. Salo, in a sense, is a follow-up to Pigsty.

In regard to the second objection, it must be noted that Pasolini's overall vision of conditions was less bleak than that hinted at in Salo, for, apparently, the film was conceived as only one part of a larger whole whose trajectory would generally parallel that of The Divine Comedy.[4] In essence, Pasolini thought of these films as one work with a trinary structure, like that of the "Trilogy of Life." As in that group of films, Salo was likely intended to deal generally with the annihilation of "physicity" (Pasolini's word), specifically in the sense that the body becomes merchandise in a consumer society of power politics which replaces the creative powers of love and individuation with the love of power and personal apotheosis.

This process begins with a desire for the "absolute" in physical and sensual experience, but as this desire becomes obsessive, living organisms are necessarily converted to objects and the "idea" of contact replaces contact itself. Abstractions are progressively substituted for living concretions, sexual arousal becomes more vicarious and self-enclosed, requiring greater distance between the subject and its object of desire (and hence greater distance between people). Domination and personal fascism define the personality; the mind turns inward on the delectation of its own physical sensations, abstracts them, and ultimately kills them in an orgy of self-destruction. Accordingly, Salo moves to an assault upon the very centers of sensitivity (eyes, tongue, nipples, etc.) and an ever greater distance between the pleasure-seeker and the object of desire. Materialism's cause and effect appear concomitant, a will to power which is an urge for oblivion.

This overview may explain why Pasolini chose to furnish this Fascist haven in Art Deco and Bauhaus styles (with, as well, paintings by Feininger, Severini, and Duchamp). First of all, the styles were popular at the time, but more significantly, the movements celebrated functionalism, industrialism, and, obliquely, man's mechanical advancements—all tributaries or features of consumerism as a philosophy. Art Deco, of course, carried the ideas into advertising—the backbone of consumerism—envisioning it as an art form. The particular logic Pasolini derives from this trend is simply that the elevation of consumerism to an art form advances the marketing of people to an art form as well, and results, eventually, in the conversion of torture and murder to aesthetic games for those in power. If this sounds absurd, one need only refer to the history of the Nazi concentration camps with their competition for "aesthetic" means of murder. (I am also reminded of the executives' decision to air a live assassination in *Network* and the Russian roulette games which loom over *The Deer Hunter*—Communist fascism producing the same perversions as consumerism.) But for Pasolini, the celebration of consumerism implicit in Art Deco (despite the appeal of its style) sanctions a national "conformism" and, thus, the death of personal conscience.

The Ante Inferno

Salo opens upon an almost sylvan scene, a quiet, green countryside dominated by a lake whose waters are quite still. This placidity, in the context of the film, presages the moral stagnation pervading *Salo*'s world. Likewise, the absence of human life in the scene is a keynote of the deprivation of healthy human qualities in the protagonists and their servants. This scene marks one of the few times in which anything associated with nature—in the common sense of "right"—is seen in the film (although Pasolini seems to see the aberrations of his characters as potentials within nature). But if not siding wholly with Rousseau's sense of the innate goodness of nature, Pasolini cinematically locates the source of evil within the social structure itself, deep within the interior of a group of buildings where our four Fascists will first be seen.

The imagistic flow of the opening shots takes us from nature to imposed structure to over-structure; we pan left from the lake to a group of typically stuccoesque Italian buildings and, finally, to the interior of these buildings, a dark, radically ordered room in which the four Fascists are seated symmetrically about a rectangular table. There are a number of important elements in this scene. Both the manner of shooting and the occupation of the characters—a ritualized signing of a pact—lends the scene an intense sense of abstraction. Ritual, itself a method of codifying behavior around a schematic model, informs and dominates the mentality of the sadists. It permeates their behavior throughout the film in their ritualistic marriages, formalized tortures, and regimented daily schedule. To emphasize the strict formality of their activity, Pasolini employs a direct frontal shot with a wide-angle lens to capture the perspectival symmetry. Equally significant is the importance placed on words by the sadists in the binding of their contract. Each figure solemnly and ritualistically signs the document, after which the first words of the film are spoken: "Everything is good in the extreme!" In the process of the film's inception, we are taken from the natural (although itself arrested) to the unnatural, defined as corruption in the heart of civilization, to an introversion of consciousness which ignores the external world through its lust for controlled abstractions. The pattern of these scenes provides a format for the process of the entire movie, a steplike journey into the heart of darkness which intensifies with each phase of the film.

Interestingly, this transition is repeated in the next scene. We move from a tranquil pool of water to three boys on bicycles, and, finally, to their capture and imprisonment. The fact that most prisoners in the film are taken while riding bicycles, or walking, underscores the Fascists' contempt for movement, for by the end of the film the very picture of a bicycle will outrage them, depicting the increasing debilitation of life in their world.

The break with nature entailed in the process of captivity is endowed with particularly perverse overtones, as we see one mother pursue her son to give him a scarf. Strangely, he tells her to "go away." There is (as Pasolini himself suggested) a dangerous will to submissiveness on the part of the captives, the allegorical equivalent to the compliance of the complete consumer in a materialistic state. They make isolated attempts to escape, but surprisingly generate no organized revolution in spite of the overt and total depravity of their captors. Perverting the Freudian imperative of growth through psychological annihilation of the parent, the Fascists literally kill parents when necessary and replace them with political authorities (a quality of all totalitarian states, whether Nazi or Stalinist).

The children are marshaled into a drab office in a scene which evokes the motifs of the opening shots. They are lined up in symmetrical fashion and ritualistically converted to abstractions in the eyes of their captors as their names are written on squares of paper and placed in a rectangular glass box for future auctioning. Again, the wide-angle lens frontal shot is used to enhance the sense of constrictive and obsessive control.

Within the main villa, the children are stripped and examined for defects. Appropriately, the only person rejected is a girl with an imperfect mouth. This oral fixation is an early symptom of the Fascists' obsession with speaking. The sadism of the libertines will be marked by their progressive assault on the mouth throughout the film: their perversion of written laws, the compulsory consumption of nails and excrement, and, finally, the abrasion of the tongue in the final tortures. Apparently, the overvaluation of language as the glue of ritual prompts concern with its "symbolic" source (the mouth), fostering its misuse and destruction (in fact, spitting on others is one of the initial forms of degradation in the film).

The most important element latent in the proceedings is the subordination of females to males, femininity to masculinity. While the captives are equally divided between boys and girls, there is a sexual division made among them. For example, we learn that girls have been used as bait to catch boys; we see that there are four female accomplices totally indentured to the four male rulers, and that among the captives the males are granted a superior status to the females, being granted sexual rights over them and being seated on chairs while the girls are normally forced to sit on the floor. In fact, prior to the end of the film, the most explicit tortures are practiced on the girls—nail eating, excrement eating, and immersion in a vat of feces. In some sense, "maleness" embodies the impulse toward absolute control and domination; "femaleness," toward emotion, creativity (narrators, parody artists, are all women), and receptiveness. The behavior of the characters dissolves the natural bond between male and female spirits, creating an evermore sterile environment. This pattern becomes quite visible in the homosexual marriages of the rulers in "The Circle of Blood," their murder of a guard and servant who attempt a heterosexual affair, and, finally, the last shot of the film, which discloses two males dancing with each other. Obsession with control and sensuality is thus defined as a progressive elimination of one half of the human personality, followed by an incestuous introversion of the male powers upon themselves.

Power becomes a narcissistic immersion in its own mirror image systematically drawing the mind away from nature and the outside world. Hence, the examination of the captives is followed by a full-scale retreat of the captors and captives to a remote fortress, the villa at Salo. As our movement becomes progressively inward, it becomes more obviously dominated by rituals, words, laws, abstractions, and males. The "Ante Inferno" closes with a solemn and pompous recitation of the laws of confinement to the captives. While the captors stand on a heavy balcony, the captives stand appropriately below them in the yard, naked. Beneath the choking blanket of perversion, however, certain natural impulses still reveal themselves; a male guard divulges a romantic attraction to a female servant (Zumurrud from *The Arabian Nights*), but both of them are later killed.

The scene concludes with the closing of the rule books and the herding of the captives to the interior of the villa: abstraction, enclosure, and interiorization define the conditions of Fascist libertinism.

Circle of the Manias

With the opening of the "Circle of the Manias" episode, the peculiar nature of the "lust for power" is manifested along two lines: self-enclosure and the replacement of direct sexual arousal with the "idea" of sexual arousal. Reality, in actual experience, is replaced by a mediated form of it. Thus, despite the casual disposal of naked bodies around the room, the four masters find it necessary to employ a female narrator to spin erotic tales for their excitement. Appropriately, each story deals with situations in which sexual arousal is achieved through a mediator; the name of the narrator, Signora Vacarri, even suggests vicariousness. This sense of mediated form replacing immediate experience is suggested by the scene's opening shots of the mirrored image of Signora Vacarri (as opposed to the "real" one) applying cosmetics.

In line with Pasolini's sense of progress, what follows in the "Circle of the Manias" is to some degree the sequential evolution of the issues inhering in the opening shots. Reality first assumes the form of the almost monolithic voice of the narrator, hence the form of "pure word." As the voice prevails, we witness a successive debasement of organic form, of people. After dinner the mediating voice is incarnated as a manikin, and in the following scene the libertines abandon whatever sense of autonomy they pretend to hold for their captives, mechanizing them in a mock marriage in which the children are reduced essentially to puppets. The idea of nuptial felicity is used as a stimulant to the sexual drives of the captors. The ceremony ends with "anal rape," a rather growing obsession of the libertines in this episode.

The nature of this obsession seems similar to that in *The Canterbury*

Salo: listening to tales in the story room

Tales, in which the substitution of mediating devices for reality becomes a process of elimination (hence the concern for the eliminatory organs). Reality is converted into excrement (which literally happens in the "Circle of Excrement"). What becomes progressively eliminated in this section of the film is the humanity of the captives, for following the mock wedding they are placed on leashes and made to behave like dogs.

The most painful event in this scene is the forced feeding of a ball of cheese filled with nails to one of the girls. Her mouth bleeds to the delight of the libertines. In one dimension, this assault on the organ of speech is an aspect of the eventual self-destruction implicit in the verbal mediation prevailing in the episode. There is a sense in which the perversion of communication inherent in the condition (self-enclosure) of the narrative must destroy its own organ. Accordingly, the final scene of the "Circle of Manias" depicts how attempts at communication between the captives have become surreptitious and indirect. Two girls try to talk only in whispers and two boys are reduced to writing with their fingers on the floor. The possibility for verbal language, in the logic of the narrative, is on the verge of disappearing.

One may also note that, in the feeding episode, the infliction of physical pain will become a substitute for sexual arousal in the libertines. This, in turn, would seem to be the logical result of the self-enclosure which characterizes the *Salo* universe, convergent in the initial image of Signora Vacarri self-absorbed in her mirror. Pain becomes the only possibility for consciousness when imagination turns inward, producing a form of "art" (the narratives we hear) which is a parody of imaginative activity rather than a realization of love or creation. It is a tool of imprisonment rather than growth.

Circle of Excrement

The "Circle of Excrement" episode seems primarily concerned with consumption and excretion, the two becoming merged in the degenerate atmosphere of the four Fascists. Consequently, the "center" scene of the episode is a large meal in which the libertines and their captives consume the excrement of the boys and girls. In some manner, this event should be seen as the logical outcome of the impulse toward power and enclosure with which the film began and as an allegory for consumerism. It represents a model of self-enclosure which has become self-consumptive, except the process has become a matter of consuming one's own excrement. Hence, although the mode of stimulation for the four masters has grown more concrete—moving from ideas to actual excre-

Salo: the captive children herded downstairs for a mock wedding

ment—the process is merely an extension of the conditions established earlier: self-enclosure, self-suffocation.

In many ways, the events of this section of the film repeat those of the former sections, and why not, for the dietary habit is a cycle of reconsuming that which has been already eaten. Experience becomes more overtly pernicious by containing even more redundancy, for indeed, enclosure, control, and enslavement allow neither the spontaneous exhibition of novelty (the game of the masters merely acts out experiences in the narrators' past) nor the openness of contact which would breed freshness and experimental change. No possibility for real change (for real love or real creation) is allowed to exist. More repetition is thus inevitable and necessary. Because of this, the "excrement episode," like the one before it, opens with one of the female chanteuse absorbed in her mirror image. Following the established format, we are taken into the story room and presented with tales of childhood perversion. Signora Matis's tale, however, leads into a discussion of matricide—an extension of the killing-off of the family begun in the "Ante Inferno"—and to what is surely the most disgusting scene in the movie, that in which a girl whose mother has been recently slain is forcibly enjoined to consume a turd freshly dropped by one of the masters.

The turd-eating becomes a prelude to another permutation of the will to control. The four masters actually set up rules and regulations for bowel movements, inspecting the chamberpots each morning for offenders. Fascism has moved from being a form of imprisonment to being a literal destruction of the body—of physicality itself, a perverse allegory of consumerism's obsession with "products."

The "Circle of Excrement" closes with an episode in which the desire for repetition is made explicit. A beauty contest for fundaments is held with the winner to receive as a prize his or her immediate execution. However, the execution proves to be a ruse, a fact explained by one of the masters: "You fool, do you think we'd kill you? We want to kill you thousands of times through all eternity." As this episode suggests, the rapaciousness of the libertines has been progressively attracted to death itself (or more accurately, the *idea* of death) as the ultimate sexual stimulant.

This episode concludes with a long story regarding a man most aroused by women who were under a death sentence ("You can't find better excrement than that from a woman who has just heard her death sentence"). In Freudian terminology, this fetish thoroughly describes the condition of the "anal complex," whose appearance in an adult provides a useful measure of his arrested growth. Thematically it suggests another gross allegorical pun vis-à-vis the nourishment of the Fascist mind through "feeding on fear." And, as well, the maniacal fascination with death clarifies the lust for personal oblivion which slumbers in the Fascist soul beneath its woolly-headed pursuit of power. Experience becomes food for destruction, death and feces its most overt "eliminatory" products.

Circle of Blood

As do the other episodes, the "Circle of Blood" opens upon people absorbed in mirror reflections. In this case, however, the usual female has been replaced by three of the libertines in drag, sedulously preening themselves. This substitution of male for female is part of the thematic process in the film involving the gradual disappearance of women, and feminine powers in general. In terms of this issue, the trajectory of the film brings it to a marriage (or a visual union) of male with male: the closing shot of the film being two Fascist guards dancing with each other.

Implicit in the urge for enslavement is a sort of onanism, or autism, a fear of connecting with others, especially maleness with its opposite (femininity and creativity). Masculine control becomes (like the four masters) self-absorbed, marrying only itself. As such, of course, it becomes more destructive, more dissociative, and, by constantly separating itself from its subjects, more distanced and abstract. In terms of Pasolini's economic situation, what we have enacted for us is a version of the classical subject/object split inherent in Western rationality. It is in terms of this development that the final scene (the dismemberment of the prisoners) makes sense.

To properly enjoy the torture, each of the masters must watch only at a great distance. Thus they sit by turns in a window of the villa remorselessly viewing the slaughter with binoculars (which seem to accentuate the unreality of the proceedings, a fact conveyed to us by Pasolini's imposition of binocular masks over his shots of the tortures). The absence of natural human feeling in all of this, as well as the desire to eliminate it from experience, is reflected by the paintings which surround the voyeurs: quasi-abstract works in which human presence is rendered insignificant in the clash of huge, stark battlefields of incompatible colors. The dehumanization germane to the art is also the goal sought by the libertines in the deliberate distancing of themselves from the murders. The action eviscerates the ferocity of the sadism so that the libertines may enjoy it on the level of abstract ritual, the mode of experience most congenial to their sensibilities. As with voyeurism, pleasure precludes contact; it even precludes unfiltered vision, immense degrees of mediation being required to ignite the sexual fantasies of the observer because it is the idea rather than the actuality which titillates. The adoration of ritualized voyeuristic experience is, alas, a sexual lust for an idea.

In addition to providing the sexual metaphors of power as masculine hegemony, the final section of the movie makes explicit a degree of complicity on the part of the captives in their own destruction, a possibility earlier suggested in one boy's abrupt dismissal of his mother. The youths betray each other in a series of confessions which implicate their fellows in crimes against the laws of the libertines. Obviously, they are driven to this extreme by the hope and primal desire for self-preservation, but the episode reveals their continued naiveté regarding the degree of perversion in their captors. The series of informings leads to the one act of rebellion at the villa. The Fascist bishop, confronting one victim after another in the string of informings, comes upon one of the guards making love with a female servant in a normal fashion. The guard refuses to cooperate and dies in a blaze of gunfire, brandishing a Communist salute. The informers whose betrayals led to discovery of the guard are rewarded with uniformly sadistic deaths.

The death of the guard and the maid forms the final act in the annihilation of heterosexual relationships implicit in the mentality of the libertines, and it is accompanied by greater emphasis on male conjunction with male. Thus the death of the guard has been preceded by an elaborately ritualized all-male wedding, the libertines assuming the female role by adorning themselves in female drag. Women, of course, have gradually disappeared from the film altogether. Their last willed acts consist either of lesbian lovemaking or suicide. The women narrators enact a parody wedding themselves, interrupting the normal ritual of storytelling with a ridiculous song-and-dance which pays tribute to the idea of paying the rent through prostitution. Soon after, the pianist, the last woman not a torture victim, jumps to her death from the story room. While both male and female children are slaughtered in the chilling finale, the general trend of the final section, according to the climate of the entire film, has been toward the elimination of femininity. This annihilation is complemented by the domination of fire rather than water (the feminine element in the film) in the film's closing tortures (most prisoners are burned). The still waters present in the opening shots have been altogether eliminated from the world of the film, along with their traditional associations with life.

Conclusion: Pasolini's Dark Vision

With this final evaporation of feminine elements and femininity itself, *Salo* concludes with a gesture that reveals the film to be the dark side of *The Arabian Nights*. Pasolini's vision of a world in which no individuality can exist, in which freedom and self-liberation are incomprehensible, divulges a terrain wholly dominated by males, all pursuing the traditional male "virtue" of manipulating people to generate social order. The world of *Salo* is precisely, even rationally, regulated, yet imbued with the hearty good cheer of a well-run gas chamber. *Salo* ends, ironically, with a vision of mercantile exploitation more distasteful and odoriferous than that of *Accatone*, but closely related to it.

As an audience, we are cheated not by the bleakness of *Salo* but by the fact that it does not embody Pasolini's real "final" vision of life, only one slumbering possibility he saw in the world. Pasolini's hunger for life, which originally inseminated his imagination, assumed a malignant disguise in *Salo*—as it did on the director's final night—but it produced, on the other hand, a unique body of works which testify to the value of an imagination so passionately committed to life.

One would like, at this juncture, to be able to summarize Pasolini's career, somehow, but that task is, at present, out of reach. With Pasolini the man, however, one can at least comment upon his distinct modernity. His sense of alienation, his homosexuality, his experiences with revolution and Marxism, his prodigious creative capacity and the brutality of his death converge to form a portrait of a man who embodies in the most visible and painful way the peculiar and distinctive characteristics of the Twentieth-century landscape. It seems to me that this total configuration of experience, which runs the gamut from self-hatred to creative fulfillment, and which forms the matrix of his cinematic art should surely increase in relevance for us in the future rather than dissolve into incomprehensibility.

Notes and References

Preface

1. *Paracriticisms* (Urbana, 1975), p. 3.
2. Paul Willeman, ed., *Pier Paolo Pasolini* (London, 1977), p. 65; hereafter cited as *PW*.

Chapter One

1. A self-portrait by Pasolini in Elio Accroca, ed., *Ritratte Su Misura di Scrittari Italiani* (Venice, 1960), p. 205, as translated by Olga Ragussa in her *Narrative and Drama* (Paris, 1976), pp. 136–37; italics mine.
2. Interview with Gideon Bachmann, "Pasolini on De Sade," *Film Quarterly*, 29, no. 2 (1975–1976), 43.
3. In 1957 he was awarded the national Viareggio Prize for his volume of poetry entitled *The Ashes of Gramsci*.
4. *Ragazzi di Vita* (Milan, 1955) and *Una Vita Violenta* (Milan, 1959). See bibliography for English language editions. Pia Friedrich discusses Pasolini's literary work in detail in *Pier Paolo Pasolini* in the Twayne World Author Series.
5. See Pasolini's essay "Why That of Oedipus is a Story" (1967), in *Oedipus Rex* (New York, 1971), pp. 8, 9, 12. Also in Oswald Stack, ed., *Pasolini on Pasolini* (Bloomington, 1970), p. 152; hereafter cited as *PP*.
6. For more details see Edith Schloss, "Pier Paolo Pasolini: Who Killed the Poet?" *Nation*, December 6, 1975, pp. 599–600; Patrick Pacheco, "The Death of a Poet," *After Dark*, 8, no. 3 (1976), 70–75.
7. *PP*, p. 14.
8. "Pier Paolo Pasolini: An Epical-Religious View of the World," *Film Quarterly*, 28, no. 4 (1965), 35; hereafter cited as *FQ*.
9. *PP*, p. 29.
10. Susan MacDonald, "Pasolini: Rebellion, Art, and a New Society," *Screen*, 10, no. 3 (1969), 26. Regarding the visitor in *Teorema* Pasolini says, "The young man does everything with a certain amount of irony, but the kind of irony which is paternal. And yet he has this almost maternal tenderness,"

interviewed by Leonard Berry, "Drunk on Reality," *Guardian* (U.K.), March 6, 1969, p. 8.

11. See "Pasolini—Press Conference, New York Film Festival, 1966," *Film Culture*, no. 42 (1966), 101: "Eating has a deeper significance than just destruction. There is also the Jungian meaning." I am only demonstrating, of course, Pasolini's familiarity with Jung's work, not his discipleship. In other essays he often employs Jung's phrase "the collective unconscious:" "Cinematic and Literary Stylistic Figures," *Film Culture*, no. 24 (1962), 42; also the dream discourse in "The Cinema of Poetry."

12. "Intellectualism . . . and the Teds," *Films and Filming,* 7 (January, 1961), 17f.

13. Raymond Durgnat discusses this in "Pasolini's Knife Edge," *New Society*, 41 (August 11, 1977), 299–300.

14. Ian Wright, interviewer, "Dialogue with Piety," *Guardian* (U.K.), December 1, 1964, p. 7.

15. Interview with John Bragin, "Pasolini—A Conversation in Rome, June, 1966," *Film Quarterly*, no. 42 (1966), 105; hereafter cited as *PCR*.

16. "Why That of Oedipus is a Story," pp. 8–9.

17. Interview with Gideon Bachmann, "Pasolini Today," *Take One*, 4, no. 5 (1973), 21; hereafter cited as *PT*.

18. *PCR*, pp. 103–5.

19. *FQ*, p. 36.

20. *PP*, p. 77.

21. *PCR*, p. 104.

22. Ibid.

23. Interview with James Blue, "Pier Paolo Pasolini," *Film Comment*, 3, no. 3 (1965), 30.

24. *PP*, p. 29.

25. "The Pesaro Papers," *Cinim*, 3 (Spring, 1969), 8.

26. *FQ*, p. 32.

27. Quoted in *Newsweek*, November 17, 1975, p. 64; italics mine.

28. *PP*, pp. 14, 77.

29. From a discussion with anonymous questioner, "Pasolini—Varda—Allio—Sarris—Michelson," *Film Culture*, no. 42 (1966), 98–99.

30. *PT*, p. 21.

31. As in his essay "The Cinema of Poetry," *Cahiers du Cinema in English*, no. 6 (1966), 34–43; conveniently reprinted in Bill Nichols, *Movies and Methods* (Berkeley, 1976).

32. "Why That of Oedipus is a Story," p. 6.

33. *PP*, p. 29.

34. *PP*, p. 153.

35. *PP*, p. 21.

36. *PCR*, p. 103.

37. *PT*, p. 21.

38. James Blue interview, p. 26.

39. Interview with Leonard J. Berry, "Drunk on Reality," *Guardian* (U.K.), March 6, 1969, p. 8; abridged in Leonard Berry, "According to Pasolini," *Commonweal*, March 7, 1969, p. 707.

40. *PCR*, p. 105.

41. *PP*, p. 152.

42. *PP*, p. 29.

43. *PW*, p. 75.

44. *PW*, pp. 77, 74–75.

Chapter Two

1. Translated by William Weaver in *Contemporary Italian Poetry*, ed. Carlo L. Colino (Berkeley, 1962), pp. 194–207.

Chapter Three

1. "Problematic" is the word Pasolini applies to the situation in an interview with Nino Ferrero: "*Mamma Roma* ovvero, dalla responsabilita individuale alla responsabilita colletiva," as printed in *Con Pier Paolo Pasolini*, ed. Enrico Magrelli (Rome, 1977), p. 45.

Chapter Four

1. See, for example, Gunnar Kumlein, "A Marxist Christ," *Commonweal*, July 2, 1965, pp. 471–72. Susan MacDonald, "Pasolini: Rebellion, Art, and a New Society," *Screen*, 10, no. 3 (1969), 26.

2. Interview with Ian Wright, "Dialogue with Piety," *Guardian* (U.K.), December 1, 1964, p. 7.

3. *PP*, p. 83: "If I had reconstructed the history of Christ as he really was I would not have produced a religious film. . . . I would have produced a positivist Marxist reconstruction. . . . I did not want to do this, because I am not interested in deconsecrating."

4. *PP*, p. 77.

5. *PCR*, pp. 103–5.

6. See John Bragin, "Pier Paolo Pasolini: Poetry as Compensation," *Film Society Review*, 4, no. 5 (1969), 12–18; 4, no. 6 (1969), 18–28; 4, no. 7 (1969), 35–40. Bragin's criticisms of Pasolini's techniques are a bit absurd and unpenetrating.

7. *PCR*, p. 104.

8. MacDonald, *Screen*, 10, no. 3 (1969), 26.

9. This is an important facet of his theory of cinema and reality and is the subject of an interview with James Blue, "Pier Paolo Pasolini," *Film Comment*, 3, no. 4 (1965), 25–32, as well as Pasolini's essay "Why That of Oedipus is a Story" in *Oedipus Rex* screenplay.

10. Pasolini says this explicitly: "If the cinema is another language, cannot

such an unknown language be based on laws which have nothing to do with linguistic laws ... ?" ("The Scenario as a Structure Designed to Become Another Structure," *Wide Angle*, 2, no. 1 [1978], 40–47).

11. *PCR*, p. 104.

Chapter Five

1. *PCR*, pp. 102–5.

2. Published as "The Scenario as a Structure Designed to Become Another Structure," p. 43.

3. Pier Paolo Pasolini, "The Pesaro Papers," *Cinim*, 3 (1969), 6–11.

4. *PP*, p. 152.

5. Pasolini stresses the irrationality of the image in "The Cinema of Poetry," *Cahiers du Cinema in English*, no. 6 (1966), 34–43.

6. *PCR*, p. 105.

7. "The Cinema of Poetry," p. 36.

8. *PP*, pp. 100, 108.

9. *PP*, pp. 22–23, 106.

10. *PCR*, pp. 103, 105.

Chapter Six

1. *PP*, p. 131.

2. *PP*, p. 124.

3. "Why That of Oedipus is a Story," p. 8.

Chapter Seven

1. *PW*, p. 68.

2. Appropriately, even in the realm of mythology, his divine ancestor is Aeolus, god of winds, providing an inheritance of change and motion.

3. Discussions of the nature and limitations of "humanism" abound: see, for example, Irwin Thompson, *At the Edge of History* (New York, 1971).

4. One might compare his end to that of Encolpio in *Fellini Satyricon*. When given the opportunity by Eumolpus to inherit the bourgeois world, he chooses instead to expand his soul through continued exploration.

Chapter Eight

1. Leonard Berry, "According to Pasolini," pp. 706–7.

2. "Why That of Oedipus is a Story," pp. 8–9.

3. See Roy Armes, *The Ambiguous Image* (London, 1976), for example.

4. Not a Christ symbol, though: "One thing I want to make clear though: the young man is not Christ! He has something of the divine but he's not Christ!" (Leonard Berry, "According to Pasolini," pp. 706–7).

5. "Post Modernity and Hermeneutics," *Boundary 2*, 5 (Winter, 1977), 363–95. See also Doris L. Eder, "*Surfiction:* Plunging into the Surface," *Boundary 2*, 5 (Fall, 1976), 153–57; Raymond Federman, ed., *Surfiction Now*

... *And Tomorrow* (Chicago, 1975); Willem Flusser, "Line and Surface," *Main Currents in Modern Thought,* 29 (January–February, 1973), 100–106. Most relevant to cinema is Stan Brakhage, *Metaphors on Vision* (New York, 1963).

6. Translated by Hazel Barnes (New York, 1966), p. 3.

7. Two rather opposite psychological treatments of this condition are Rollo May, *Love and Will* (New York, 1969) and B. F. Skinner, *Beyond Freedom and Dignity* (New York, 1971).

8. John Bragin, "Poetry as Compensation, Part Three," *Film Society Review,* 4 (March, 1969), 36.

Chapter Nine
1. *PT*, p. 21. "One of the least appetizing things of the past few years are precisely those fashionable political films, these fictional political films, which are the films of half truths, of reality-unreality, of consolation and falseness."

2. *PP*, p. 142.

3. See the Introduction; also, for an interesting though different treatment of the theme, Noel Purdon, "Pasolini: The Film of Alienation," *Cinema* (U.K.), August, 1970, pp. 14–21, reprinted in *PW*.

4. *PP*, pp. 11–14; Pasolini notes, "A great deal of my erotic and emotional life depends not on hatred for my father but on love for him. . . ."

Chapter Ten
1. *PT*, p. 21.

2. *PT*, p. 20.

3. *PT*, p. 19.

4. There is some confusion about whether Pasolini is Giotto or Giotto's pupil in the film, but the screenplay identifies him as Giotto, the pupilage a part of his disguise.

5. I am indebted to Ben Lawton, "Theory and Praxis in Pasolini's Trilogy of Life: *Decameron,*" *Quarterly Review of Film Studies,* 3 (1977), 400, for this observation as well as his identification of the Breughel paintings. Lawton supplies a detailed discussion of the framing, particularly in regard to the source of the stories in Boccaccio's original and to those parts invented by Pasolini.

6. See Lawton's essay referred to in the above note

Chapter Eleven
1. A different version of this essay was published with Allison Graham as coauthor, entitled "Pasolini's *The Canterbury Tales:* The Fall of the Bourgeois Artist," in *1978 Film Studies Annual* (Purdue, 1978), pp. 1–9.

2. *PW*, p. 70.

3. "Why That of Oedipus is a Story," p. 7.

Chapter Twelve

1. *PW*, p. 77.

2. *PW*, pp. 74–75, "Destiny itself, understood however as normality, as the essence of every occurrence and human condition. . . . the antagonists not named in normal destiny are in fact magic and homosexuality."

3. A very fine review essay which treats this aspect of the film is Albert Benderson, "Pasolini's *Arabian Nights:* A Review," in *1976 Film Studies Annual* (Purdue, 1976), pp. 211–14. Notes Benderson perspicaciously, "In *The Arabian Nights* . . . it is love not sex which is the ultimate mystery."

Chapter Thirteen

1. Pasolini interviewed by Gideon Bachmann, "Pasolini on De Sade," *Film Quarterly*, 29, no. 2 (1975–1976), 39–45.

2. "Pasolini on De Sade," pp. 40, 41.

3. Roland Barthes, "Pasolini's *Salo:* Sade to the Letter," in *PW*, pp. 64–66.

4. See "Pasolini on De Sade" and Bachmann's other discussions of the film with Pasolini, "The 220 Days of 'Salo,'" *Film Comment*, 40 (1976), 38–47, and "Pasolini and the Marquis De Sade," *Sight and Sound*, 45 (Winter, 1975–1976), 50–54.

Selected Bibliography

· 1. Interviews

a. Book-length interviews

MAGRELLI, ENRICO, ed. *Con Pier Paolo Pasolini*. Rome: Bulzoni, 1977. A very useful collection of interviews plus a long essay by Pasolini on Fellini. This can be purchased in the United States through S. F. Vanni, Publishers and Booksellers, 30 W. 12 St., New York 10011.

STACK, OSWALD. *Pasolini on Pasolini*. Bloomington: Indiana University Press, 1969. Probably the best primary source on Pasolini in English or Italian.

b. Short interviews (translated into English); arranged chronologically

LANE, JOHN FRANCIS. "The New Realists of Italy: Five Directors." *Films and Filming*, 7, no. 4 (1961), 20–21. Pasolini with Bolognini and others speaks briefly about his works.

DE GRAMONT, SANCHE. "Pier Paolo Pasolini." *New York Herald Tribune*, November 22, 1964. Pasolini explains his interest in the Christ of Matthew.

WRIGHT, IAN. "Dialogue with Piety." *Guardian* (U.K.), December 1, 1964, p. 7. Pasolini discusses how *The Gospel According to Matthew* criticizes Marxism.

"Pier Paolo Pasolini: An Epical-Religious View of the World." Translated by Letzilia Miller and Michael Graham. *Film Quarterly*, 28, no. 4 (1965), 31–45. Pasolini answers questions submitted by students at the Centro Sperimentale di Cinematographica in Rome.

BLUE, JAMES. "Pier Paolo Pasolini." *Film Comment*, 3, no. 4 (1965), 25–32. Blue's interview concentrates on Pasolini's methods of handling actors.

"Pasolini—Varda—Allio—Sarris—Michelson." *Film Culture*, no. 42 (1966), 96–100. Pasolini discusses his distinction between a cinema of poetry and a cinema of prose.

"Pasolini—Press Conference New York Film Festival, 1966." *Film Culture*, no. 42 (1966), 101–2. Pasolini fields questions about the symbolism in his films.

BRAGIN, JOHN. "Pasolini—A Conversation in Rome, June, 1966." *Film Culture*, no. 42 (1966), 102–5. The best early interview with Pasolini, in which he discusses the relationship between spirituality and Marxism in his films.

"Symposium, Pier Paolo Pasolini." *Arts in Society*, 4, no. 1 (1967), 72–76. Pasolini discusses the major influences on his films and responds to such questions as "What is the prime quality needed by a good filmmaker?"

BERRY, LEONARD. "Drunk on Reality." *Guardian* (U.K.), March 6, 1969, p. 8; partly reprinted in Leonard Berry, "According to Pasolini," *Commonweal*, 89 (March 7, 1969), 706–7. Pasolini talks of *Teorema* and filmmaking quite colorfully.

BACHMANN, GIDEON. "Pasolini Today." *Take One*, 4, no. 5 (1973), 18–21. Illuminating interview regarding Pasolini's changing attitudes about life, film, and politics.

―――. "Pasolini on De Sade." *Film Quarterly*, 29, no. 2 (1975–76), 39–44. Pasolini discusses De Sade and his film *Salo*.

―――. "Pasolini and the Marquis De Sade." *Sight and Sound*, 45, no. 1 (1975–1976), 50–54. Largely repeats material in preceding entry.

―――. "The 220 Days of *Salo*." *Film Comment*, 40, no. 2 (1976), 38–47. A memoir by the author in diary format which includes conversations with Pasolini.

"Pasolini on Film." In *Pier Paolo Pasolini*, edited by Paul Willeman, pp. 67–77. London: British Film Institute, 1977. Previously unavailable interviews with Pasolini on his films *Medea*, *The Decameron*, *The Canterbury Tales*, and *The Arabian Nights*. Useful supplement to Oswald Stack's book.

c. Essays on cinema (translated into English); arranged chronologically

"Intellectualism. . . and the Teds." *Films and Filming*, 7, no. 4 (1961), 17f.

"Cinematic and Literary Stylistic Figures." *Film Culture*, no. 24 (1962), 42–43. Metaphor cannot literally exist in cinema as it does in literature. Essay reprinted in *Interviews with Film Directors*, ed. Andrew Sarris (New York: Avon, 1967).

"The Cinema of Poetry." *Cahiers du Cinema in English*, no. 6 (1966), 34–43. A difficultly worded essay in which Pasolini promotes his antiverbal semiology of the natural sign and discusses Antonioni's *The Red Desert*.

"The Scenario as a Structure Designed to Become Another Structure." Translated by Michele de Cruz-Saenz. *Wide Angle*, 2, no. 1 (1977), 40–47. Originally published in *Uccellacci e Uccellini* (Milan: Garzanti, 1966). Suggests film semiotics must be totally extricated from assumptions of verbal linguistics.

"Why That of Oedipus is a Story." Translated by John Mathews. In *Oedipus*

Rex. Modern Film Scripts. New York: Simon and Schuster, 1971. Pp. 5–
    13. Originally pubished in *Edipo Re* (Milan: Garazini, 1967). Revealing
    essay in which Pasolini detaches himself from "Marxist Freudian dogma"
    and the semiology of Metz, proposing his own "natural sign" views.
"The Pesaro Papers." Anonymous translator. *Cinim*, no. 3 (1969), 6–11. Orig-
    inally delivered at Pesaro Film Festival, June, 1968. Stresses subjectivism
    of all perception in which one point of view may undermine the reliability
    of another as truth.

2. Literary Works available in English

a. Novels

The Ragazzi (*Ragazzi di Vita*, 1955). Translated by Emile Capouya. New
    York: Grove Press, 1968.
A Violent Life (*Una Vita Violenta*, 1958). Translated by Bruce Kupelnick.
    New York: Garland, 1978.

b. Poetry

"A Desperate Vitality." Translated by Norman MacAfee and Luciano Marti-
    nengo. *Christopher Street*, June, 1977, pp. 24–29.
"Apennine" ("L'appennino"). Translated by William Weaver. In *Contempo-
    rary Italian Poetry*, edited by Carlo Golino, pp. 194–207. Berkeley: Uni-
    versity of California Press, 1962.
"Part of a Letter to the Codignola Boy." Translated by Gavin Ewert. In *Italian
    Writing Today*, edited by Raleigh Trevelyan, p. 54. Baltimore: Penguin
    Books, 1967.
"Something's Always Missing." *Italian Writing Today*, p. 55.
"To a Pope." Translated by Robert Connolly. *Film Comment*, 3, no. 4 (1965),
    24.

Secondary Sources

1. Bibliographies

LAWTON, BEN. *Pier Paolo Pasolini: A Guide to References and Resources*. Bos-
    ton: G. K. Hall, 1980. Thorough bibliography covering European and
    American criticism.
"Pier Paolo Pasolini." *Bianco e Nero*, 1, no. 4 (1976). The entire issue is
    devoted to Pasolini with a detailed bibliography.

2. Books

WILLEMAN, PAUL, ed. *Pier Paolo Pasolini*. London: British Film Institute, 1977.
    Although it purports to present analyses of Pasolini's films, outside of Pur-
    don's essay there is little film analysis. Instead, the collection concentrates
    more on his semiotics and homosexuality. Most essays are reprints. The

collection includes, however, otherwise inaccessible interviews with Pasolini which supplement those in Oswald Stack's *Pasolini on Pasolini:* Geoffrey Nowell-Smith, "Pasolini's Originality"; Don Ranvaud, "De-Liberate Evil"; Antonio Costa, "Pasolini's Semiological Heresy"; Noel Purdon, "Pasolini: The Film of Alienation"; Richard Dyer, "Pasolini and Homosexuality"; Roland Barthes, "Pasolini's *Salo:* Sade to the Letter."

3. Essays

ARMES, ROY. "Pier Paolo Pasolini: Myth and Modernity." In *The Ambiguous Image*. London: Secker and Warburg, 1976. Pp. 154–64. A general discussion of Pasolini's use of pastiche; has little to do with myth.

BENDERSON, ALBERT. "Pasolini's *Arabian Nights:* A Review." In *1976 Film Studies Annual*. Purdue, 1976. Pp. 211–14. An excellent discussion of the sexual politics of the film.

BRAGIN, JOHN. "Pier Paolo Pasolini: Poetry as Compensation." *Film Society Review*, 4, no. 5 (1969), 12–18; 4, no. 6 (1969), 18–28; 4, no. 7 (1969), 35–40. A review in three parts of Pasolini's career. The discussion of *Teorema* is especially interesting. Bragin does not believe in footnotes.

DURGNAT, RAYMOND. "Pasolini: Equivocations of the Androgyne." In *Sexual Alienation in the Cinema*. London: Studio Vista, 1972. Pp. 209–42. This long essay deals with *Teorema* and *Oedipus Rex*. Durgnat is seldom boring and often insightful, although he tends to stray far afield from the films.

———. "Pasolini's Knife Edge." *New Society*, 41 (August 11, 1977), 299–300. An interesting review of Pasolini's career.

ECO, UMBERTO. "Articulations of the Cinematic Code." In *Movies and Methods*, edited by Bill Nichols, pp. 591–604. Berkeley: University of California Press, 1976. A critical interpretation of Pasolini's semiotics as barbarously worded as Pasolini's essays.

GOUGH-YATES, KEVIN. "Pier Paolo Pasolini and the 'Rule of Analogy.'" *Studio International*, March, 1969, pp. 117–19. A haphazard collection of observations on Pasolini's films, mainly regarding his pictorial allusions to other painters and filmmakers, that is occasionally illuminating.

KAUFFMANN, STANLEY. "Poet and the Pimp." *New Republic*, April 6, 1968, p. 22. A fine review of *Accatone*.

LAWTON, BEN. "Theory and Praxis in Pasolini's Trilogy of Life: *Decameron*." *Quarterly Review of Film Studies*, 3 (1977), 395–415. Provides an enlightening discussion of Pasolini's *The Decameron* through comparison to Boccaccio's original. Also provides a precis of each of Pasolini's theoretical essays.

MACDONALD, SUSAN. "Pasolini: Rebellion, Art, and a New Society." *Screen*, 10, no. 3 (1969), 19–34. Provides useful biographical information and a discussion of Pasolini's novels and films through *Teorema*.

PURDON, NOEL. "Pasolini: The Film of Alienation." *Cinema* (U.K.), 6, no. 7

(1970), 14–21. A discussion of *Pigsty* and *Teorema* in a generally psychological vein.

SCHLOSS, EDITH. "Pier Paolo Pasolini: Who Killed the Poet?" *The Nation*, December 6, 1975, pp. 599–600. An account of Pasolini's murder and its murky details.

STEVENS, M., and GILBERT, S. "Death Imitates Art." *Newsweek*, November 17, 1975, p. 64. An account of Pasolini's murder.

TAYLOR, JOHN RUSSELL. "Pier Paolo Pasolini." In *Directors and Directions: Cinema for the Seventies*. New York: Hill and Wang, 1975. Pp. 44–69. An overview of Pasolini's career.

Filmography

Many of Pasolini's short films are unavailable; listed below are primarily his feature-length films.

ACCATONE (Cino del Duca-Arco Film, 1961)
Producer: Alfredo Bini
Assistant director(s): Bernardo Bertolucci, Leopoldo Savona
Screenplay: Pier Paolo Pasolini, with special dialogue collaboration by Sergio
   Citti
Cinematographer: Tonino Delli Colli (b/w)
Art Director: Flavio Mogherini
Music: J. S. Bach, coordinated by Carlo Rustichelli
Sound: Luigi Puri, Manilo Magara
Editor: Nino Baragli
Cast: Franco Citti (Accatone/Vittorio), Franca Pasut (Stella), Silvana Corsini
   (Maddelena), Paola Guidi (Ascenza), Adriana Asti (Amore), Mario Cipri-
   ani (Balilla), Umberto Bevilaqua (Don Salvatore), Roberto Scaringelia
   (Cartagine)
Accatone's voice: Paolo Ferrari
Running time: 120 minutes
U.S. Premiere: September 17, 1966; New York Film Festival
16mm rental: MacMillan/Audio-Brandon, Mt. Vernon, N.Y.

MAMMA ROMA (Arco Film, 1962)
Producer: Alfredo Bini
Assistant director: Carlo di Carlo
Screenplay: Pier Paolo Pasolini, dialogue collaboration by Sergio Citti
Cinematographer: Tonino Delli Colli (b/w)
Art Director: Flavio Mogherini
Set Decoration: Massimo Tavazzi
Music: Vivaldi, coordinated by Carlo Rustichelli
Sound: Leopoldo Rosi
Editor: Nino Baragli

187

Cast: Anna Magnani (Mamma Roma), Ettore Garofolo (Ettore), Franco Citti
(Carmine), Silvana Corsini (Bruna), Luisa Loiano (Biancofiore), Paolo
Volpini (Priest), Luciano Gonnini (Zacaria)
Running time: 110 minutes
U.S. Premiere: No acknowledged screening
16mm rental: No U.S. distribution; Gala in Great Britain

LA RICOTTA (One episode in ROGOPAG, other episodes directed by
Roberto Rossellini, Jean-Luc Godard, Ugo Gregoretti; Arco Film-Cineriz,
1962)
Producer: Alfredo Bini
Assistant director: None
Screenplay: Pier Paolo Pasolini
Cinematographer: Tonino Delli Colli (b/w and color)
Art Director: Flavio Mogherini
Set Decoration: Massimo Tavazzi
Costumes: Danilo Donati
Music: Popular rock 'n' roll, Verdi ("Always Free," from La Traviatta, selec-
tions from Rigoletto), coordinated by Carlo Rustichelli
Sound: Leopoldo Rossi
Editor: Nino Baragli
Cast: Orson Welles (the Director), Mario Cipriani (Stracci), Laura Betti (the
Star), Edmondo Aldini (another Star), Vittorio La Paglia (the Journalist),
Ettore Garofolo (an Extra), Maria Bernardini (Extra who does striptease)
Director's voice: Giorgio Bassani
Running time: 40 minutes
U.S. Premiere: September, 1963; New York Film Festival
16mm rental: MacMillan/Audio Brandon

The script for La Ricotta—a forty-minute episode in the compilation film
Rogopag—was written during the shooting of Mamma Roma, yet in tone
seems as far removed from that work as does Fellini's 8½ from i Vitelloni.
The Felliniesque style of La Ricotta seems, in fact, a deliberate parody of
Fellini's work, particularly of 8½, which was released in 1962 (somewhat
before Mamma Roma).

Pasolini's story is a humorous fable about a subproletarian extra, Stracci, who
dies from overeating when, after losing or giving away his lunch (rationed by
the company), he is fed by the workers in a grotesque parody of the Last Supper. His tribulations go largely unnoticed by the director, who sits with total
artistic detachment from his crew. In fact, he hardly moves throughout the
film.

The allusions to Fellini are particularly strong in the final scenes of the film.
The producer has arranged an outdoor banquet to promote the director's religious film and the placement of the tables seems closely modeled on the ban-

quet setup in 8½ (the long, white-clothed tables are reminiscent in each case of the Last Supper).

Pasolini's director, played by Orson Welles, is interviewed during a break by a reporter who has sneaked onto the set. One of the questions he poses is the director's opinion of Fellini, to which Welles replies with detachment, "He dances." Then, with a particularly interesting quirk, Pasolini turns Welles into a parody of himself, having the director read the poetry (rather self-obsessed and plaintive verse) which Pasolini wrote and published in the screenplay of *Mamma Roma*.

Whether Pasolini's satire is aimed at Fellini, himself, or both of them, it centers mainly on the disregard of the director for the problems of the poor while pursuing his personal aesthetic goals, the achievement of artistic freedom at the cost of ignoring the more gritty sufferings of the common man. Such, indeed, is the kind of criticism Marxists are prone to aim at 8½, since the creative problems encountered by Guido seem far removed from the struggle to earn a living which occupies the lives of most men. The argument could be contested with Pasolini's own weapons (that the life of the body is dead without the life of the spirit), but that is another topic.

LA RABBIA, FIRST PART (Opus Film, 1963, second part by Giovanni Guareschi)
Producer: Gastone Ferrante
Script: Pier Paolo Pasolini
Commentary spoken by: Giorgio Bassani, Renato Guttuso
Editor: Nino Baragli
Running time: 50 minutes
16mm Rental: Warner Brothers
The film was withdrawn by Warners immediately because of Guareschi's episode and has never been commercially released anywhere since.

La Rabbia (The Frenzy) is composed entirely of documentary material. Pasolini claims not to have shot a single frame. The newsreel footage deals with the Algerian war, Pope John, and the return of Italian prisoners of war from Russia. Pasolini composed poetry and commentary which is delivered by his friend, Giorgio Bassani, the writer, and Renato Guttuso. The tone is that of Marxist denunciation. Pasolini felt the only thing in his part of the film worth keeping was a sequence devoted to the death of Marilyn Monroe. Pasolini's part was coupled with another episode, directed by Giovanni Guareschi, of the opposite side of the political spectrum. Racist overtones of this part, however, caused the film to be blocked.

THE GOSPEL ACCORDING TO MATTHEW (Arco Film—Rome, C.C.F. Lux—Paris, 1964)
Producer: Alfredo Bini

Executive Producer: Manolo Bolognini
Assistant Director: Maurizio Lucidi
Screenplay: Pier Paolo Pasolini
Cinematographer: Tonino Delli Colli (b/w)
Art Director: Luigi Scaccianoce
Costumes: Danilo Donati
Music: Original score by Luis Enriquez Bacalov, other selections include Congolese "Missa Luba," Bach's *St. Matthew Passion*, "Sometimes I Feel Like a Motherless Child" sung by Odetta, and pieces from Mozart and Weburn.
Sound: Mario Del Pezzo
Special Effects: Ettore Catallucci
Still Photography: Angelo Novi
Editor: Nino Baragli
Cast: Enrique Irazoqui (Christ), Margherita Caruso (the Young Mary), Susanna Pasolini (the old Mary), Marcello Morante (Joseph), Mario Socrate (John the Baptist), Settimo di Porto (Peter), Otello Sestili (Judas), Ferruccio Nuzzo (Matthew), Giocomo Morante (John), Alfonso Gatto (Andrew), Enzo Siciliano (Simon), Giorgio Agamben (Philip), Guido Cerretani (Bartholomew), and a cast of hundreds.
Christ's voice: Enrico Maria Salerno
Running time: 140 minutes
U.S. Premiere: February 17, 1966; New York
16mm rental: Continental Distributing, Inc. Also rental and lease: MacMillan/Audio-Brandon

SOPRALUOGHI IN PALESTINA PER 'IL VANGELO SECONDO MATTEO' (Arco Film, 1963–1964)

Producer: Alfredo Bini
Cameraman: Aldo Pennelli
Speakers: Pier Paolo Pasolini, Don Andrea Carraro
Commentary: Pier Paolo Pasolini
Running time: 50 minutes
Never distributed commercially anywhere
Edited and commented on by Pasolini for the VIII Spoleto Festival, July, 1965

Sopraluoghi in Palestina per "Il Vangelo Secondo Matteo" (On location in Palestine for "The Gospel According to Matthew") is not really a Pasolini film. The footage was taken by the cameraman, Aldo Pennelli, largely according to his own taste and edited by an unnamed laboratory technician by request of Alfredo Bini who wanted to provide material to potential distributors. Pasolini wrote the commentary.

COMIZI D' AMORE (Arco Film, 1964)
Producer: Alfredo Bini
Production Manager: Eliseo Boschi
Commentary written by: Pier Paolo Pasolini
Commentary spoken by: Lello Bersani and Pier Paolo Pasolini
Directors of Photography: Mario Bernardo, Tonino Delli Colli
Camera Operators: Vittorio Bernini, Franco Delli Colli, Cesare Fontana
Editor: Nino Baragli
Cast: Pier Paolo Pasolini, Cesare Musatti, Giuseppe Ungaretti, Susanna Paso-
lini, Camilla Cederna, Adele Cambria, Oriana Fallaci, Antonella Lualdi,
Graziella Granata (and, suppressed in the editing, Giuseppe Ravegnani
and Eugenio Montale)
Locations: Palermo, Calabria, Naples, the Po Valley and various sites through-
out Italy
Running time: 90 minutes
16mm Rental: Titanus (Italy); never shown commercially in Britain or U.S.

Comizi d' Amour (Assembly of Love) is one of Pasolini's feature-length films
not covered in this book (the other is *Orestia Africanus*). At the time of this
writing the film had not been subtitled for English speaking audiences and is
not likely to be for some time. As the film is composed entirely of interviews
and commentary its value is radically restricted to any but an Italian audience,
as Pasolini admits: "Someone who does not know Italian properly could not
take the film in" (*PP*, p. 65). Its role in the development of his fictional narrative is probably of less importance than was that of *La Ricotta*.

Pasolini interviews a cross-section of Italian society from children in the
Palermo slums to a Bologna football team, speaks with Oriana Fallaci and
Alberto Moravia. Between discussions of politics and homosexuality, he exam-
ines the structure of the Italian family, concluding with shots from a real wedding at which he reads his own poetry.

THE HAWKS AND THE SPARROWS (Arco Film, 1966)
Producer: Alfredo Bini
Assistant Directors: Sergio Citti and Vincenzo Cerami
Screenplay: Pier Paolo Pasolini
Cinematographers: Tonino Delli Colli and Mario Bernardo
Art Director: Luigi Scaccianoce
Set Director: Vittorio Biseo
Costumes: Danilo Donati
Music: Ennio Moricone, song by Amedeo Cassola
Sound: Pietro Ortolani and Armando Bondani
Editor: Nino Baragli
Cast: Toto (Innocenti Toto/Brother Ciccillo), Ninetto Davoli (the Son, Inno-

centi Ninetto/Brother Ninetto), Femi Benussi (Luna), Rossana Di Rocco
(friend of Ninetto), Lena Lin Solaro (Urganda), Rosina Moroni (Peasant
Woman), Renato Capogna and Pietro Davoli (Medieval Louts), Gabriel
Baldini (Dante's Dentist)
Voice of the Crow: Francisco Leonetti
Running time: 91 minutes
U.S. Premiere: September, 1966; New York Film Festival
16mm Rental: MacMillan/Audio-Brandon

LA TERRA VISTA DALLA LUNA (Dino De Laurentiis Cinematografica,
1966; episode in **LE STREGNE;** other episodes by Luchino Visconti,
Mauro Bolognini Vittorio De Sica, Franco Rossi)
Assistant Director: Sergio Citti
Script: Pier Paolo Pasolini
Director of Photography: Giuseppe Rotunno
Color Process: Technicolor
Costumes: Piero Tosi
Sculptures: Pino Zac
Editor: Piero Piccioni
Cast: Toto (Ciancicato Miao), Ninetto Davoli (Basciu Miao), Silvana Mangano
(Assurdina Cai), Laura Betti (Tourist), Luigi Leone (Tourist's Wife),
Mario Cipriani (priest)
Running time: 20 minutes
Location: Rome and surroundings (Fiumicino)
U.S. Premiere: 1969; not yet shown commercially in Britain
16mm Rental: Dear Film/United Artists (Italy), Lopert (U.S.)

Pasolini considered *la Terra Vista dalla Luna (The Earth seen from the
Moon)* to be one of his most successful pieces. The film was motivated by
Pasolini's desire to use Toto and Ninetto (from *The Hawks and the Sparrows*)
in a story which did not smother their comic gifts with ideology. The story
concerns Toto as a deaf and dumb protagonist who participates in a miracle
of sorts in which Sylvana Mangano is transformed.

CHE COSA SONO LE NUVOLE (Dino De Laurentiis Cinematografica,
1966; episode in **CAPRICCIO ALL' ITALIANA;** other episodes by
Steno, Mauro Bolognini (2), Pino Zac, Mario Monicelli)
Producer: Dino De Laurentiis
Script: Pier Paolo Pasolini
Director of Photography: Tonino Delli Colli
Editor: Nino Baragli
Song: "Cosi sono le Nuvole": Domenico Modugno and Pier Paolo Pasolini
Color Process: Technicolor
Cast: Toto (Iago), Franco Franchi (Cassio), Ciccio Ingrassia (Roderigo),

Domenico Modugno (Dustman), Ninetto Davoli (Othello), Laura Betti (Desdemona), Adriana Asti (Bianca), Carlo Pisacane (Brabantio), Francesco Leonetti (Puppeteer)
Running time: 20 minutes
U.S. Premiere: Not yet shown commercially in Britain or U.S.
16mm Rental: Euro International Films (Italy)

Che Cosa Sono Le Nuvole (What are Clouds) is another short piece centered on Toto and Ninetto. The one features a group of puppets who come to life briefly after being taken to a junkyard. They perform for a subproletarian audience.

LA FIORE DI CAMPO (Castoro Film, Anouchka Film, 1967; episode in **AMORE E RABBIA;** other episodes directed by Lizziani, Bertolucci, Godard, Bellocchio)
Director of Photography: Guiseppe Ruzzolini
Color Process: Technicolor
Music: Giovanni Fusco
Editor: Nino Baragli
Cast: Ninetto Davoli
Running time: 12 minutes
Not available for rental.

La Fiore Di Campo (The Flower in the Piazza) is one long tracking shot of Ninetto Davoli walking along the Via Nationale in Rome with three other shots cut in. While Ninetto strolls along carrying a large papier-mâché flower other images dealing with wars and world tensions are inserted to construct a picture of him as a somewhat mindlessly happy lad, blissful only by virtue of his innocence. In the middle of a traffic jam he hears the voice of God prompting him to wake-up. Unfortunately he fails to comprehend and must die.

OEDIPUS REX (Arco Film, 1967)
Producer: Alfredo Bini
Assistant Director: Jean-Claude Biette
Screenplay: Pier Paolo Pasolini, inspired by Sophocles' *Oedipus Rex* and *Oedipus at Colonus*
Cinematographer: Giuseppe Ruzzolini (Technicolor)
Art Director: Andrea Fantacci
Costumes: Danilo Donati
Music: *Quartet in C Major* by W. A. Mozart, Rumanian folksongs, ancient Japanese music, coordinated by Pier Paolo Pasolini
Sound: Carlo Tarchi
Editor: Nino Baragli

Cast: Franco Citti (Oedipus), Sylvana Mangano (Jocasta), Alida Vali (Merope), Carmelo Bene (Creon), Julian Beck (Tiresias), Luciano Bartoli (Laius), Francesco Leonetti (Laius's slave), Ahmed Bellachmi (Polybus), Giandomenico Davoli (Polybus's shepherd), Ninetto Davoli (Angelo, the boy guide), Pier Paolo Pasolini (High Priest)
Running time: 110 minutes
U.S. Premiere: No acknowledged screening
16mm rental: None known in U.S. (including 35mm)

TEOREMA (Aetos Film, 1968)
Producers: Franco Rossellini and Manolo Bolognini
Assistant Director: Sergio Citti
Screenplay: Pier Paolo Pasolini
Cinematographer: Giuseppe Ruzzolini (Eastman Color)
Art Director: Luciano Puccini
Costumes: Marcella De Marchis
Music: *Requiem* by W. A. Mozart, performed by the Moscow Philharmonic Orchestra and choir of the Russian Academy; original score by Ennio Moricone, Bruno Nicolai
Sound: Dino Fronzetti
Special Pictorial Advisor: Giuseppe Zigaina
Editor: Nino Baragli
Cast: Terence Stamp (the Visitor), Sylvana Mangan (Lucia), Massimo Girotti (Paolo), Anne Wiazemsky (Odetta), Laura Betti (Emilia), Andre Jose Cruz (Pietro), Ninetto Davoli (Angelino), Susanna Pasolini (Old Peasant), Alfonso Gatto (Doctor)
Running time: 93 minutes
U.S. Premiere: April 21, 1969; New York
16mm rental: Continental Distributing, Inc. Also available from Budget Films (Los Angeles) and Kit Parker Films (Carmel Valley, Calif.)

MEDEA (San Marco Films/Rosima Anstaldt—Rome, Les Films Number One—Paris, and Janus Films/Fernsehen—Munich, 1969)
Producers: Franco Rossellini and Marina Cicogna
Assistant Director: Carlo Carunchio
Screenplay: Pier Paolo Pasolini, inspired by Euripedes' *Medea*
Cinematographer: Ennio Guarnieri (Eastman Color)
Art Directors: Dante Ferretti and Nicola Tamburino
Costumes: Piero Tossi
Music: Folk and classical, supervised by Pier Paolo Pasolini, Elsa Morante
Editor: Nino Baragli
Cast: Maria Callas (Medea), Massimo Girotti (Creon), Giuseppe Gentili (Jason), Laurent Terzief (the Centaur), Margareth Clementi (Glauce), Anna Maria Chio (Nurse)

Running time: 118 minutes
U.S. Premiere: September, 1971; New York
16mm rental: New Line Cinema (New York)

APPUNTI PER UNA ORESTIADE AFRICANA (Baldi, 1969)
Producer: Jan Vittorio Baldi
Screenplay: Pier Paolo Pasolini
Director of Photography: Giorgio Pelloni
Editor: Nino Baragli
Running time: 70 minutes
For rent only in 35mm from Bauer Film International

Despite the availability of this film, it has, to my knowledge, never been shown commercially in America as of the writing of this book. The film recounts a tale of lost spirit, based upon the *Orestiade*, intermingled with discussions with modern African students. The story of the Furies is treated as an allegory on the modern situation of the Africans—a people in transition from a mythological to a rational mentality, pursued by the apparition of their lost past. Pasolini shows the assumption of the consciousness involved with rational technology must create a spiritual crisis. The similarity of the story to that of *Medea*, filmed only shortly before, is quite obvious.

PIGSTY (Film dell'Orso/Idi Cinematographica/I.N.D.I.E.F.—Rome, C.A.P.A.C.—Paris, 1969)
Producer: Gian Vittorio Baldi
Associate Producer: Gianni Barcelloni
Assistant Directors: Sergio Citti and Fabio Garriba
Screenplay: Pier Paolo Pasolini
Cinematographers: Tonino Delli Colli, Armando Nannuzzi, Giuseppi Ruzzolini
Art Director: Danilo Donati
Costumes: Danilo Donati
Music: Benedetto Ghiglia
Sound: Alberto Salvatore
Editor: Nino Baragli
Cast: Pierre Clementi (Cannibal), Jean Pierre Leaud (Julian), Alberto Leonello (Klotz), Ugo Tognazzi (Herdhitze), Anne Wiazemsky (Ida), Margarita Lozano (Frau Klotz), Marco Ferreri (Hans), Franco Citti (second Cannibal), Ninetto Davoli (Young Man/Marracchione)
Running time: 100 minutes
U.S. Premiere: August, 1975; New York
16mm rental and sale: New Line Cinema

THE DECAMERON (Produzione Europee Associate—Rome, Les Productions Artistes Associes—Paris, and Artemis Films—Berlin, 1971)

Producer: Alberto Grimaldi
Executive Producer: Franco Rossillini
Associate Director: Sergio Citti
Assistant Director: Umberto Angelucci
Screenplay: Pier Paolo Pasolini, based upon Boccaccio's *Il Decameron*
Cinematographer: Tonino Delli Colli
Art Director: Dante Ferretti
Set Decoration: Andrea Fantacci
Costumes: Danilo Donati
Music: Pier Paolo Pasolini with Ennio Morricone
Sound: Pietro Spadoni
Editors: Nino Baragli, Tatiana Morigi
Cast: Franco Citti (Ciappelletto), Ninetto Davoli (Andreuccio), Angela Luce
    (Peronella), Patrizia Capparelli (Alibech), Jovan Jovanovic (Rustico),
    Gianni Rizzo (Head Friar), Pier Paolo Pasolini (Giotto), Silvana Mangano
    (Madonna), Monique Van Vooren (Queen of Skulls), Elizabetta Davoli
    (Caterina)
Running time: 111 minutes
U.S. Premiere: October, 1971; New York Film Festival
16mm rental: United Artists 16

THE CANTERBURY TALES (P.E.A.—Rome, 1972)
Producer: Alberto Grimaldi
Assistant Directors: Sergio Citti, Umberto Angelucci, Peter Shepherd
Screenplay: Pier Paolo Pasolini, based on Chaucer's *The Canterbury Tales*
Cinematographer: Tonino Delli Colli
Art Director: Dante Ferretti
Set Decoration: Kenneth Muygleston
Costumes: Danilo Donati
Music: Ennio Morricone, historical selections coordinated by Pier Paolo
    Pasolini
Sound: Primimiano Muratore
Editor: Nino Baragli
Cast: Pier Paolo Pasolini (Chaucer), Hugh Griffith (January), Josephine Chaplin
    (May), Laura Betti (the Wife of Bath), Ninetto Davoli (the Cook's appren-
    tice), Franco Citti (the Devil), George Datch (Host of the Tabard), Daniel
    Buckler (Summoner), Michael Balfour (John the Carpenter), Jenny Run-
    acre (Alison), Dan Thomas (Nicholas)
Running time: 111 minutes
U.S. Premiere: January, 1975; New York
16mm rental: None. 35mm rights held by United Artists

THE ARABIAN NIGHTS (United Artists Europe, 1974)
Producer: Alberto Grimaldi
Assistant Directors: Umberto Angelucci and Peter Shepherd

Screenplay: Pier Paolo Pasolini, from *The Thousand and One Nights*
Art Director: Dante Ferretti
Costumes: Danilo Donati
Music: Ennio Morricone
Sound: Luciano Welisch
Editors: Nino Baragli and Tatiana Morigi
Cast: Inez Pellegrine (Zumurrud), Ninetto Davoli (Aziz), Franco Citti (the Demon), Franco Merli (Nur ed Din)
Running time: 130 minutes
U.S. Premiere: March, 1976; Purdue University First Annual Conference on Film
16mm rental: None. 35mm prints at one time available from United Artists

SALO, OR THE ONE HUNDRED AND TWENTY DAYS OF SODOM
(P.E.A.—Rome, P.A.A.—Paris, 1975)
Producer: Alberto Grimaldi
Assistant Director: Sergio Citti
Screenplay: Pier Paolo Pasolini with Sergio Citti, based upon *120 Days of Sodom* by the Marquis de Sade
Cinematographer: Tonino Delli Colli
Art Director: Dante Ferretti
Costumes: Danilo Donati
Music: Ennio Morricone
Editor: Nino Baragli
Cast: Paolo Bonacelli (Duke), Giorgio Cataldi (Bishop), Umberto P. Quinavalle (Magistrate), Aldo Valletti (President), Caterino Boratto (Signora Castelli), Elsa De Giorgi (Signora Maggi), Helene Surgere (Signora Vaccari), Sonia Savlange (Virtuosa)
Running time: 117 minutes
U.S. Premiere: October 8, 1977; New York Film Festival
16mm rental: None. 35mm prints from Peppercorn Wormser, New York

Index

DATE DUE
